HUGH MACDIARMID

Black, Green, Red & Tartan

HUGH MACDIARMID

Black, Green, Red & Tartan

Bob Purdie

Welsh Academic Press

Published in Wales by Welsh Academic Press, an imprint of

Ashley Drake Publishing Ltd
PO Box 733
Cardiff
CF14 7ZY

www.welsh-academic-press.com

First Impression – 2012

ISBN
978-1-86057-027-8

British Library Cataloguing-in-Publication Data.
A CIP catalogue for this book is available from the British Library.

Typeset by White Lotus Infotech Pvt. Ltd., Puducherry, India.
Printed by MPG Book Group Ltd, Bodmin, Cornwall

CONTENTS

For Sean, Dale, David, Daniel,
Stuart, Owen and Kirsty

Abbreviations

Æ	George Russell
BBC	British Broadcasting Corporation
CP/C.P.	Communist Party
CPGB	Communist Party of Great Britain
H.M.M.	H. M. Murray
ILP	Independent Labour Party
NPS	National Party of Scotland
NEP	New Economic Policy
SA	Sturmabteilung
SNL	Scots National League
SHRA	Scottish Home Rule Association
SNP	Scottish National Party
UK	United Kingdom
USSR	Union of Soviet Socialist Republics

Introduction

I'll ha'e nae hauf- way hoose, but aye be whaur
Extremes meet - it's the only way I ken
To dodge the curst conceit o' bein' richt
That damns the vast majority o' men.[1]

(From *A Drunk Man Looks at the Thistle*)

Hugh MacDiarmid was a man in constant revolt, against a stiflingly narrow Scottish culture, against all that was provincial and philistine in Scottish society and against Scotland's dependency on England. He believed that the Scottish culture of his day was making the nation satisfied with its subordinate status within the UK and he strove for a self-reliant and independent, European, nation. He succeeded in shaking up many of the accepted norms of Scottish culture and he is recognised as a having made a major contribution to twentieth century literature, through his poetry.

He was born in the Borders town of Langholm in 1892 and began his political life on the left. He joined the Independent Labour Party and the Fabian Society in Edinburgh before the First World War. In Montrose, where he worked as a journalist, he was an Independent Socialist Councillor, a Justice of the Peace, and a member of the No More War Movement – the British section of War Resisters International. He was a lifelong Scottish nationalist and a supporter of Social Credit, the financial reform scheme proposed by his friend Major Douglas. In 1923 he published two articles that have been interpreted as endorsing fascism, but the titles are misleading, he never was a fascist. He joined the Communist Party of Great Britain in 1934 and remained a Communist and a Scottish nationalist for the rest of his life.

A staple argument about MacDiarmid is that he was contradictory and the above political biography might be taken as proof. How could he seem to endorse fascism and then, ten years later, become a Communist? How did he reconcile Marxism and Social Credit? Why did he believe that Communism was compatible with Scottish nationalism? Were his ideas hopelessly confused? Another cliché is that he was unreasonable. But we should distinguish between his often intemperate polemics and the substance of his political thought. He challenged the consensus of, what he argued, was a culturally mediocre Scotland and he was regarded as unreasonable for doing so by many of his contemporaries, therefore dismissing his politics assumes that that prevailing wisdom of his day was right.

This book will argue that his political ideas do make sense, which does not imply that they could have been successful. He was bad at politics, he lacked patience and awareness of how other people thought, he alienated potential allies and he did not explain himself effectively, even to his friends, and he often blamed his meagre success on the stupidity and perfidy of others. But these faults are not uncommon in strong minded people who make a mark on their times, and they are not an excuse for a failure to examine his political ideas.

MacDiarmid was not only a great poet, he was also highly intelligent and well-read. In 1980 Neal Ascherson predicted,

It looks as if the man read what he quoted, and – for example in philosophy and aesthetics – mastered the systems which lie behind these endless references. There are books coming which will make MacDiarmid look even taller."[2]

The books have not appeared and MacDiarmid stature has probably diminished. But Ascherson's other claim was right, MacDiarmid did read what he quoted and he did grasp the systems of their writers. But he did so in a highly individual way. He read a great deal in the 1920s and '30s because he supplemented his earnings as a journalist from book reviews and he received "heaps of books for review – generally books of an *avant garde* character ..."[3] These reviews were written in the midst of a hectic literary, political and family life, so he read quickly and absorbed ideas in deep gulps.

In 1954 he was gently joshed by his friend Moray McLaren about his claims to have absorbed vast swathes of international culture, despite not reading the languages of much of the literature on which he expressed opinions. He replied,

I determined long ago not to learn every language, but to acquire such a body of knowledge and understanding that I could see the poetical output of mankind as a whole and know what every sizeable poet 'stood for' and 'amounted to' in relation thereto, no matter in what language. ...[4]

Brian Smith's account of MacDiarmid's life in Shetland confirms this. His assistant, Grant Taylor, remembered that MacDiarmid did not have a, "formal knowledge of the languages he delighted to quote", but when Taylor had been, "... struggling doing a literal translation ...

trying to get at the idea ... and he would say 'Oh yes!' ... and his mind had jumped ahead of mine ... ."[5]

His intuitive grasp of a text meant that, without detailed study, he was able to compose an overview of the culture and ideas of writers from a number of different societies. But the haste with which he did so meant that he incorporated into his writings his own misinterpretations, although sometimes with creative results. And, because he had no time for such niceties, he reproduced ideas and whole passages from his reading without bothering about scholarly referencing and probably without remembering where he got them.[6]

Some readers may think that my use of MacDiarmid's writings is perverse. I have analysed very little of his poetry, while his prose writings, some of them fairly ephemeral, are examined in detail. That is because this is a work of political history, not of literary criticism. And that is also the reason for much of the book not being directly about MacDiarmid. I believed that it was necessary to provide background information on political movements and schools of thought that were important for him, but are less familiar in our day. And I have tried to follow up his references to now forgotten authors and to read what he was reading. I hope that, in this way, I have been able to explain some controversial or puzzling aspects of his political ideas. My contention is that he makes much more sense when his political ideas are seen in historical context, as he responded to new ideas and new challenges.

This book is not a biography and it follows a thematic, not a strictly chronological order. There are five chapters, "Black," discusses his relationship to fascist and right wing ideas in the mid 1920s. "Green," looks at his involvement with Social Credit and explains its significance for him. "Tartan," examines his participation in Scottish nationalist politics in the 1920s and '30s. "Red" analyses his Marxism and his relationship with the Communist Party of Great Britain in the 1930s. Finally "Red and Tartan" will consider his politics during and after the Second World War.

I am indebted to the existing scholarship on MacDiarmid, my work stands on the shoulders of the critics and biographers who have written about him and who are listed in the references and bibliography. I owe a great deal to Alan Riach and the other editors of the Carcanet volumes of MacDiarmid's writings. Without their work I could never have undertaken the huge amount of original research that would have been required. And a great deal of my research was signposted by the Carcanet texts.[7]

I am grateful for their assistance to the staffs of the Bodleian Library (Oxford), the British Library (London), the British Library of Political and Economic Science (London), the University of Delaware Library

(Newark, Delaware, USA), Edinburgh Central Library, Edinburgh University Library, the Mitchell Library (Glasgow), the National Library of Ireland (Dublin), Ruskin College Library (Oxford) the National Library of Scotland (Edinburgh) and the Scottish Poetry Library (Edinburgh).

Thanks are due to Terry Cradden (Derry), Owen Dudley Edwards (Edinburgh), Stephen Howe (Oxford), Scott Meikle (Glasgow), Adrian Moore (Oxford), Mike Rooke, (Nottingham) and the late James D. Young (Falkirk) all of whom read and commented on different drafts at different times. I owe a special debt of gratitude to John Manson (Castle Douglas), who generously shared with me the results of his own researches, sometimes producing precisely the document I needed at a particular time. And thanks to Paul O'Leary of Aberystwyth who proposed the idea of this book and commented on early drafts.

My twin brother, David C. Purdie, was establishing his reputation as a Scottish poet during the writing of the book and I have benefited from many discussions with him about Scotland and Scottish culture. Edna and Michael Longley and Eamon Hughes in Belfast have been supportive friends throughout. Roy Foster, Stephen Howe, David Norbrook and Tom Sherry in Oxford encouraged me to believe that my work was important. Finally, I am grateful to Richard Budd of Somerset, the book dealer who started it all off by selling me my copy of MacDiarmid's *Albyn*. Needless to say, only I should be held responsible for what is written here.

I have added, as an appendix, MacDiarmid's review of Odon Por's *Fascism*. This is a key text for understanding his politics, which has not previously been recognised and is not part of the published corpus of his political writings.

Bob Purdie
Kirkcaldy,
November 2011

Notes

1. Hugh MacDiarmid, *Complete Poems,* Vol. I, Manchester, Carcanet, 1993, p. 87.
2. "MacDiarmid and Politics", in P. H. Scott and A. C. Davis, *The Age of MacDiarmid*, Edinburgh, Mainstream, 1980, p. 225.
3. *Raucle Tongue, The III,* p. 539.
4. *Scottish Journal* No.4, Christmas 1952.
5. Brian Smith, "Stoney Limits, the Grieves in Whalsey" in Laurence Graham, and Brian Smith (eds.), *MacDiarmid in Shetland*, Lerwick, Shetland Library, 1992.
6. Peter McCarey makes much the same point in his *Hugh MacDiarmid and the Russians*, Scottish Academic Press, Edinburgh, 1987, pp. 196–7.

7. Hugh MacDiarmid, *Albyn Shorter Books and Monographs*, Manchester, Carcarnet, 1996, edited by Alan Riach. Hugh MacDiarmid, *The Raucle Tongue. Hitherto Uncollected Prose*, Vol. I, Manchester, Carcarnet, 1996; Vol. II, 1997; Vol. III, 1998, edited by Angus Calder, Glen Murray and Alan Riach. MacDiarmid, Hugh, *Hugh MacDiarmid, Selected Prose*, Carcarnet, Manchester 1992, edited by Alan Riach. Hugh MacDiarmid, *Lucky Poet*, Manchester, Carcarnet, 1994, edited by Alan Riach. Hugh MacDiarmid, *New Selected Letters*, Manchester, Carcarnet, 2001, edited by Dorian Grieve, Owen Dudley Edwards and Alan Riach.

1

Black

MacDiarmid and Fascism

T. S. Eliot – it's a Scottish name –
Afore he wrote 'The Waste Land' s'ud h a'e come
To Scotland here. He wad ha'e written
A better poem syne – like this, by gum!

(From *A Drunk Man Looks at the Thistle*)[1]

For our day the most difficult aspect of MacDiarmid's politics is his apparent support for fascism in the early 1920s. But much comment about this seems to be based on no more than the titles of two articles, "Plea for a Scottish Fascism," and "Programme for a Scottish Fascism", published in June 1923. There is no doubt that he was influenced by right wing ideas in the 1920s, but his political writings do not show a consistent trend of fascist thought. The articles were written as fascism was just beginning to take shape and there is a bitter legacy of war and mass murder between us and the 1920s, when MacDiarmid and his contemporaries were trying to fit fascism into their existing political categories.

If these two articles had never been published it is unlikely that anyone would have thought of MacDiarmid as a fascist. He could not have joined Oswald Mosley's *British* Union of Fascists which, in any case, was not founded until 1932. In 1923 the main representatives of that ideology were the "British Fascists", right wing conservatives who had copied their name and uniforms from Mussolini's movement. Only a few small branches were established in Scotland, under the leadership of the Earl of Glasgow.[2] They were accused of providing blackleg labour to Dundee docks during the General Strike,[3] at a time when MacDiarmid was supporting the strikers in Montrose.

From Red to Black

MacDiarmid began his political life on the left. He joined the Independent Labour Party and the Fabian Society in Edinburgh in 1908. A letter from South Wales, in 1911, shows him as a typical socialist propagandist of the period, speaking in the open air and relying on wit and repartee to attract and hold an audience.[4]

> Forging ahead aye! I have already been instrumental in forming four new branches of the ILP down here. In Tredegar a policeman took my name and address on the grounds that it was illegal to speak off the top of a soap-box.
>
> I asked him if a match box was within the meaning of the Act and he put something down in his note-book ... However as a branch of 25 members was the result, I can afford to be generous.[5]

The ILP's critique of capitalism and its vision of a socialist future drew on an eclectic range of thinkers. They included utopians like Robert Owen and William Morris, conservative anti-capitalists like John Ruskin and Thomas Carlyle and ethical thinkers like Edward Carpenter and RH Tawney. Alongside it the Fabian Society sought to translate this vision into practical policies, to be achieved through the state, which they saw as a benign instrument for social reconstruction. It was implicit in their thinking that a new, well ordered, society would be created and led by an enlightened elite, not by the masses. Socialists who wanted socialism to put the workers in power began to think about revolution from below. As GDH Cole put it, socialism was being reinterpreted to, "make it a more complete and balanced doctrine ... that will make democracy more really effective economically as well as politically."[6] Fabian socialism was turned upside down and the initiative for the creation of a new society was transferred to the workplace.

During his time in South Wales, MacDiarmid worked for a miners' newspaper. He lost the job because he published "extremist articles" that offended the officials of the Miners' Federation.[7] None of his journalism has survived, but it is possible to reconstruct his experiences – which he described as a "hurricane of mental and moral anarchy".[8] South Wales was experiencing an intense wave of strikes, in which rank and file miners defied their leadership. Radical Marxist ideas and Syndicalist propaganda were penetrating the ILP in the Welsh coalfields.[9] During these months MacDiarmid read the Marxist journal *Justice,* he met Keir Hardie and Tom Mann, who was a leading

Syndicalist, and he visited Ruskin College in Oxford where the Welsh students, "were of course *au fait* with Marxist doctrines".[10]

He also remembered meeting Denis Hird, the Principal of Ruskin College.[11] By 1911 Hird was actually the Warden of the Central Labour College, which had broken away two years earlier, following a dispute with the Ruskin authorities over the syllabus.[12] The students created the Plebs League through which they advocated Syndicalist ideas[13] which had a big influence on the miners of the Welsh valleys:

> The role the College and the League were to play and the influence they exercised over the educational and political development of the institutes and libraries cannot be overemphasised. The first tangible expression of this influence was the publication in 1912 of *The Miners' Next Step* by the largely Mid Rhondda based Unofficial Reform Committee whose links with the Labour College and the Plebs League were close and vital.[14]

MacDiarmid was in a crucial place at a significant time in which socialist ideas were beginning to melt and flow in the heat of class and ideological struggles. He was meeting people who were intimately connected with the forging of Guild Socialism, a new ideology which, like Syndicalism, sought a society based on federated workers' councils, organised from the shop floor upwards.

One of the main vehicles for this movement was the literary and political review *The New Age,* with which MacDiarmid was associated. In its pages not only socialism, but the distinction between left and right, was becoming plastic and malleable.

> … what began as a distrust of Socialist and Liberal objectives ended with a rejection of the ideology upon which these objectives were based. Cultural conservatism has usually been associated with reactionary politics in our century; T . E. Hulme, T. S. Eliot, and Wyndham Lewis are the three writers most often cited to illustrate this relationship. One of the unique achievements of *The New Age* was to combine a conservative theory of value with a progressive political philosophy known as Guild Socialism.[15]

Some *New Age* writers were conservatives who became more conservative, a few moved further to the left, while others worked their way through Guild Socialism and its offspring Social Credit, to a rejection of socialist ideas. Some were influenced by fascism. MacDiarmid was reading all these writers and he became a passionate advocate of Social Credit. That is why, by 1923, we should expect him to have travelled a similar journey to that of the other *New Age* intellectuals. He did so, but in unique and unexpected ways that will be explained in this and the next chapter.

The Po Marshes

His biographer, Alan Bold, claimed that the two "fascist" articles showed the:

> ... interest he had in common with some of the writers he respected most: Pound, Yeats, Wyndham Lewis; all egoists with an elitist outlook. Moreover, he dissociated himself from reactionary romanticism, saying (in 1968), 'I was friendly with both [Eliot and Yeats] but not with many of their ideas that were of a pro-Fascist character.' Consistency, after all, was the least of MacDiarmid's concerns.[16]

The writers cited by Bold had different positions on fascism and all, apart from Pound, eventually resiled from their pro-fascist views. And the terms "elitism", "reactionary romanticism" and "fascism" are conflated in a way that is unhelpful. This means that Bold was unable to explain the 1923 articles.

MacDiarmid's own defence did not clarify matters. In 1968, challenged by Hamish Henderson, he replied, "I was in the early twenties over-impressed by Italian Fascism, largely because of the draining of the Po marshes, just as others believed that Hitler in Germany did well in abolishing unemployment there." [17] When Duncan Glen asked him about Ezra Pound, he denied that the American poet had been a fascist:

> Most of my friends were fascists in that sense. They were impressed in the early days by the actual practical achievements of Mussolini in draining the Po marshes and so on, and in partially at any rate solving the unemployment problem in Italy. Now that was a temporary thing. Mussolini's real objectives became clearer later on with the invasion of Abyssinia and so on. Well none of us would have supported Mussolini in that ...[18]

This became a stock answer and he gave an almost identical reply to the Irish broadcaster Micheál Ó hUanacháin, when interviewed in 1978.[19]

Henderson pointed out that the drainage was of the Pontine, not the Po, Marshes and that the date of the scheme was 1932, nine years after the publication of "Plea for a Scottish Fascism"[20]. MacDiarmid was confused about the details but his defence was more robust than it appears. In November 1928 the *Scots Independent* noted that the Italian government was proposing a vast land reclamation scheme with the aim of feeding an extra ten millions from home produced resources. The newspaper approved, "Something of this nature is wanted in Scotland, and we shall view with interest Mussolini's experiment."

MacDiarmid, like many others, must have remembered the scheme as a positive aspect of the regime, but neither he nor Henderson referred to a crucial fact. The 1923 articles made no mention whatsoever of the Po, the Pontine, or any other marshes. In fact they contained no reference to Mussolini's social and economic policies. The two writers had focussed on an issue which seemed to be significant from the Marxist perspective they shared in the 1960s, but we need to look in an entirely different direction in order to understand what the articles really meant.

In 1923 MacDiarmid was responding to Italian Fascism just after it had come to power. The regime claimed to be a third way between *laissez faire* capitalism and state socialism and it used propaganda techniques that are familiar today, but were novel in the 1920s. This led to widespread credulity about its pretensions. In 1923 Italy was in an interregnum, the violent seizure of power had occurred in October 1922 but the suppression of all remaining opponents and the imposition of a totalitarian dictatorship did not come until 1925, after the murder of the Socialist Deputy Giacomo Matteotti in June 1924. Only at this point did it become clear that the brutality used in seizing power was more than a passing phase.

> ... Mussolini did not exactly conquer power in an altogether revolutionary manner. He was invited by the King to assume office.... Nor was parliament technically overridden. On the contrary the overwhelming majority of liberal deputies and senators agreed on giving dictatorial powers to Mussolini.... Both liberals and Christian Democrats were glad to join his cabinet.[21]

Henderson pointed out that the articles were written eight months after the March on Rome, "at a time when reports of beatings-up and castor oil dosings were causing much public concern throughout Europe ...".[22] But by the time MacDiarmid wrote his articles, the regime's watchwords had become stability and order. The Blackshirts had been transformed into a state controlled militia and the Fascist movement had become a bureaucratic political party. Italy seemed to be a moving away from counter-revolutionary violence towards constitutional rule and legality.

An Experiment in Patriotic Socialism

The sheer novelty of Italian Fascism, and its rapid mutations, made it difficult to comprehend, so two books which appeared in 1923 had a significant influence on MacDiarmid. They were *The Fascist Movement in Italian Life* by Pietro Gorgolini and *Fascism,* by Odon Por.[23] These authors made fascist ideas available in English for the first time and both argued that Italian Fascism had a left-wing potential.

Odon Por was a Hungarian who had lived in Florence since 1903 and claimed to be "not a Fascist but a Guildsman," (i.e. a Guild Socialist)[24]. He had been the London correspondent of the Italian socialist newspaper *Avanti* and was a contributor to *The New Age*. His *Syndicalism in Action,* published in 1914, was a study of the seizure of their industry by Italian glass blowers in 1910, it is still recognised as a classic work on the Syndicalist movement. He dedicated the English edition of *Fascism* to its translator Emily Townshend, who was a Fabian and a Suffragette. It bore the imprint of the Labour Publishing Company, which also brought out the Marxist journal *Labour Monthly*. It could easily be taken for a left wing book by an established socialist author.

Por saw Fascism as a fulfilment of the ideas of the Irish writer and thinker George Russell (known by his pen name Æ), who was a pioneer of agricultural co-operation. In his *The National Being, Æ* had advocated "a national civilisation brought about by means of a democracy, freely discussing its own laws – an economic democracy that will recognise a hierarchy of function and will be led by an aristocracy, not of birth, but of intellect and character."[25] (The word "function" is a key one, as will be explained in the next chapter.) Por claimed that Fascism combined the dictatorial and militarist method of Machiavelli with Russell's social reconstruction methods.[26]

Por drew parallels between Italy and the Soviet Union. Under Lenin's New Economic Policy elements of the free market had been restored, particularly in agriculture, and it seemed as if the revolution was going into reverse. Fascism, Por claimed, was going through a similar process of moderation – but in the opposite direction. It was now moving left and shedding its "White Guard", or anti-proletarian, aspects. Por quoted from Mussolini,

> The Revolution of Moscow, having first got rid of the people who were in the way by putting them to death, fell on the [state] machine and smashed it to atoms. The pendulum swung to the other extreme; now it has begun to swing back. The Fascist Revolution ... is proceeding step by step, a bit at a time. So it

happens that Moscow has to retrace its steps while Rome goes steadily on from its point of departure.[27]

Fascism, Por argued, would enable many of the traditional aspirations of socialism to be achieved. He forecast that it would "probably develop into a kind of National Socialism characterised by Guild tendencies … rather than Collectivism." It had, "… destroyed, not Socialism but its methods, setting free the living and constructive principle within from the shackles of an inert system. It has opened up for Socialism – if only the Socialists will see it – fresh horizons."[28] (Hitler's party was less than three years old and "National Socialism" referred to a socialism that was national instead of international in outlook, a common idea of the time).

When Æ reviewed Por's book, he saw Fascism as a revival of the old Roman form of dictatorship – a temporary phase, after destruction by war or civil strife, in which a single leader is given the authority to re-impose order and lay the foundations of a new state. Such a dictator would then surrender power and make way for a constitutional government. He believed that Fascism was doing no more than, "using force to bring about an efficient organisation of the Italian democracy and Italian political institutions", after the chaos brought about by class strife. But he not think that a similar revolution was needed in Ireland. [29]

Another reviewer was the Scottish journalist R. T. Clark. He also saw fascism as a temporary response to civil strife and agreed with Por that its internal logic would lead it back to its left-wing origins:

A national programme … must in the end fall foul of the interests. Mussolini's socialism is not dead, it is simply not the socialism of the official party. But the ideal he represents is precisely that which official socialism in its internationalism and defeatism deserted – the supremacy of the state, which to Mussolini is not the bureaucracy but the people.… Official socialism had ceased to be patriotic. It had put theory above the nation. Mussolini reverses that order – that is all. His is an experiment in patriotic socialism.[30]

Gorgolini was more explicit than Por about Fascist anti-communist violence. He argued that this had been a legitimate response to the chaos created by the mass strikes and factory occupations which broke out after the War, nevertheless, "Fascism is still young and is turning to the Left, for it has too many young men in its ranks who are determined to fashion the destiny of the country according to immortal principles of justice, to find a home on the Right."[31] Now it was, "time for it to exercise a propaganda of reason and persuasion, and not of violence; it must convince the heart, and not break the head."[32]

MacDiarmid reviewed both books, he quoted from Por,

> ... the origin of Fascism and its present orientation indicate that it has no desire to oppose Labour, but aims first at reconciling Labour with the nation, and secondly, at creating a national spirit of citizenship, with Labour for its basis.

He also referred to the Hungarian's,

> ... parallel between Russian Bolshevism and Italian Fascism, "just as orthodox revolutionaries are in Italian Fascism a purely conservative force, so do plutocrats see in Bolshevism one that is purely destructive. But the processes of history do not develop according to theoretical formulae, nor lend themselves to be neatly catalogued under a single heading ... the most varied types of property and of productive organisation must be recognised, but they must be framed and incorporated in a State, functioning effectively in the collective interest.... "[33]

He was even more emphatic than Clark about the left-wing potential of fascism and, in an editorial on the annual conference of the Scottish Co-operative Wholesale Society in *The Scottish Nation* of June 1923, (the issue in which his "Plea for a Scottish Fascism" appeared), he gave another perspective:

> Co-operation is essentially practical – the commercial application of that Fascism which, in other connections, would be no mere "Middle Class League" reacting against Communism, but a reaction against theoreticalism, against doctrines that take no count of facts, against illusive catch words and parrot cries. Against any attempt to run a country by the guidance of precedent or mere shibboleths.

This reflected Odon Por's view that fascism was an application of the co-operative ideas of Æ and MacDiarmid saw it as a synthesis of socialism and nationalism which might offer an alternative to the dogmatic anti-nationalism of the Scottish socialists.

Scottish Nationalists and Fascism

Other Scottish nationalists were writing the same kind of thing. Ruaraidh Erskine of Mar wrote of "a political philosophy so pregnant of meaning, so provocative to fortune, and so fertile of interest as

Fascism" but, "... how this diffusion of Italian influence is to be brought about, whether by peaceful means and measures or otherwise, has not so far been disclosed". Erskine, an aristocratic Highland Catholic, was impressed when Fascism trumpeted its "corporations" as an application of Papal social teaching, but he reserved judgement, probably because the regime had yet to mend its fences with the Vatican. And he saw no need for fascist methods in Scotland, "... an armed attempt to impose Fascism on Scotland would be resented and resisted ... On the other hand peaceful diffusion of the cultural influence of Fascismo would be ... warmly welcomed".[34]

Others, following Por, saw Mussolini's Italy through the prism of the Russian Revolution which, under Stalin, had adopted the doctrine of "socialism in one country". As "G. D." wrote in the *Free Man*:

> I do not suggest that Stalin is consciously nationalist; what I do suggest ... is that circumstances have forced him to be ... as nationalist as Mussolini or Hitler ... Whether one's objective be Communism, Fascism, or real working democracy, it will never be established save by national effort and within the confines of one country. They that wait on "international action" die disappointed like Lenin. And some Stalin, Hitler or Mussolini, someone who appeals to national instincts ... arises to do the thing the others could not realise.[35]

These Scots thought they were observing a process, which they assumed was inherent in all revolutions, for an early radical phase to be supplanted by pragmatism and moderation, as the new leaders grappled with the realities of government.

By the time Hitler had seized power in 1933, Scottish nationalists were treating the Fascist and Nazi regimes with greater scepticism. In an editorial of April 1st the *Free Man* noted revelations about the financing of the Nazi Party: "It has become clear to Hitler that ... the Nazi Party is in a dilemma, which is even further complicated by the absence on his own part of any deep understanding and the assured purpose born of it". Comment became more critical as the Nazi revolution gathered pace, although there was still confusion. In June 1933 a correspondent in the *Scots Independent* wrote that although it was "healthy and right", to feel disgust for militarism, book burnings and the persecution of Jews and Marxists, these were the "stunt moves of the Hitler-Goering group, who at present ride the Pegasus of the Germanic revival." They should be distinguished from Nazism itself, which was a "salutary revolt against the oppressive and rotten internationalism of the Central Banks".

In July 1933 a *Free Man* reader living near Dresden, who had experienced the Nazi take-over at first hand, wrote about the fear of secret denunciation and arbitrary arrest.[36] And Nannie K. Wells, a friend and collaborator of MacDiarmid's, denounced Mussolini and fascism with contempt:

> Every fresh revelation of the origin of both Fascisti and Nazi organisations show that the money on which they were reared comes from great capitalistic sources and that means also militarist sources. Both had their first origins in Socialism, borrowed the sheep's clothing to attract the flock and when they had gathered the multitude together betrayed them.... A time of heart-searching – of courageous decision, of endurance, of determined resistance to these false ideals awaits all Free Men. Maybe it is for them that our Scotland has lain fallow these years – so that within us, Leadership and Liberty – may again be reconciled as they have been more than once in our history as a nation.[37]

Like the others, in 1923 MacDiarmid had only limited knowledge of what was happening in Italy and Germany. He saw fascism as a form of left-wing nationalism and the Por and Gorgolini books reinforced this perception. But his enthusiasm waned, as evidence mounted about the real nature of the Mussolini and Hitler regimes.

Plea for a Scottish Fascism

Nevertheless, "Plea for a Scottish Fascism" and "Programme for a Scottish Fascism" must be examined, to try to discern any fascist content. In the first of the essays he asked, "Has Italian Fascism any motives or methods Scottish Nationalists may profitably borrow, or any lessons to give us?" But he warned "no doubt at first glance readers of my title will conceive of Fascism as something quite other than that to which I would seek to direct their attention."[38]

This was his starting point for a series of loosely connected ideas about contemporary Scotland. The Home Rule movement, he wrote, had been criticised for having a preponderance of socialists in its ranks and some Labour MPs were becoming ardent Scottish Nationalists. This was significant because "Scotland today is tinder awaiting the spark of genius to become ablaze with a new national consciousness and will."

He saw a long running struggle on the Hebridean island of Lewis as an example of the coming together of the nationalist and socialist ideals. The island had been purchased by the soap magnate Lord Leverhulme, who intended to develop it and to bring industrial employment to the inhabitants. But the islanders wanted land for crofting and, in a series of land raids, local crofters, many of whom had served in the war, occupied land and worked it without legal title.[39] Three Red Clydeside MPs, James Maxton, David Kirkwood and Campbell Stephen visited Lewis and MacDiarmid saw this as evidence that their experience of Westminster had led them to become nationalists.

He quoted Gorgolini's claim that:

Fascism ... is in origin an ex-combatants' movement ... Scottish Fascism may well have a similar origin – although the difference in national psychology and circumstances ... will naturally produce very dissimilar results ... It is good news that Messrs Maxton, Campbell Stephen, Kirkwood and their colleagues are to raise the West Highland land question at Westminster. The recent visit of the three named to Lewis may mark a great turning point in the history of Scottish nationalism. ... Scottish Fascism will spring naturally from the left ... and its immediate enemies are not the 'Bolshies' in our midst, but the bourgeoisie ...[40]

He agreed with R. T. Clark about the left wing potential of fascism and called on other ex-servicemen to join in breaking an "immoral" law:

Is it not time for a Scottish fascism to oppose the anti-international forces which are robbing Scotland of the finest elements of its population – and at one and the same time denying the Scottish people access to millions of acres of the finest scenery in Scotland ...? Is it not time to smash the laws which sanction and ensure such things? It can be done as soon as the *Scottish people ... think fit, without so much as asking leave of Westminster ... Rights are not asked: they are taken.*[41]

He quoted R. T. Clark, "what Fascism has achieved is *a transformation of values replacing material values by moral ones* ...."[42] The terms "spiritual" and "will" echo Fascist rhetoric, but MacDiarmid did not use the word "state" as Mussolini did. The Italian dictator wrote, "It is not the nation that generates the State .... Rather the nation is created by the State, which gives to the people conscious of its own moral unity, a will and therefore an effective existence"[43]. For MacDiarmid it was the other way round, the nation existed prior to the state and it continued to exist even when it had no state of its own.

In another passage he seems to have been influenced by the syndicalist militancy he had seen in South Wales:

> Every unemployed young Scotsman today should get out of the cities and get to the Highlands – to the vast spaces which they are forbidden to enter on pain of interdict and *squat* there ... it would be a sight for the god to see the British navy massed outside Stornoway, blockading the island, while thousands of squatters simply sat tight. If that happened ... the ex-servicemen would win and Scottish history would enter on a less humiliating phase. We want a Scottish Fascism which shall be, where such laws are concerned a lawless believer in law – a rebel believer in authority. We would substitute a new national will for these contemptible enactments of traitor legislators.[44]

The sentence "lawless believer in law – a rebel believer in authority" did express important themes of fascism – revolutionary action in defence of tradition, ideas and action which are at once destructive and conservative, the nation personified as a single will. But these were not MacDiarmid's words, they were an unattributed quote from Gorgolini's book,[45] which he had used for its vivid imagery. This was an example of his plagiarism, not of his ideology.

He went on to praise Mussolini's declaration on the rights of soldiers:

> It is not too late for Scotland to give a new, just and true promise to its soldiers and keep it: and if there are men in Scotland today realistic enough and virile enough, let them so act too that they can say: "We defend the honour and the traditions of Scotland. No one can prevent Fascists from speaking what they think. Our reigning politicians are mere comedy players. Their policy is base and fallacious. Fascism creates an atmosphere in which the nation can breathe."[46]

The passage in quotation marks was another quote from Gorgolini,[47] but for MacDiarmid it had a very different significance. The Lewis land raiders were not alienated ex-servicemen, like the Blackshirts and the SA, they were citizen former soldiers, who were rooted in a traditional community and way of life. MacDiarmid's support for them was entirely consistent with the ILP socialism of his pre-war years.

Programme for a Scottish Fascism

In his, "Programme for a Scottish Fascism," published in the July edition of *The Scottish Nation*, he stressed that he did not advocate adoption of the Italian system but only some of its aspects. He wanted the "spirit" of Italian Fascism to be moulded to the different psychology of Scotland. He believed there was a need for a new national will to overcome Scotland's inability to get its wrongs righted and he saw the potential for this in a combination of the Labour Movement and the new Scottish cultural movements. The Labour Movement, he said:

> ... is already modifying its Socialism as Mussolini modified his. It has got out of the rut of mere theory and takes service as the touchstone of social values. As soon as it ceases to work for "Socialism" and makes its goal "Scottish Socialism", it will have purged itself of the elements which make for false progress and be within measuring distance of complete triumph.[48]

Writing about the Scottish Renaissance, he referred to the Home Rule agitation of the "Red Clydeside" Labour MPs:

> To a great extent the preponderance of Labour MPs for Scotland is an aspect of the post-war recrudescence of nationalism – a reversion to type, significant less of a wide-spread demand for a new social order than of a reawakening of the traditional spirit of Scotland which was always democratic to a degree, and in a way, unknown in England. The extent to which the Labour movement can continue to effectively embody that spirit to a greater extent than any other party may depend on the extent to which Scottish Socialism develops a Fascist rather than a Bolshevik spirit – and puts nationalism (the service of the nation as a whole) first.[49]

His dichotomy of "Fascist" and "Bolshevik" was less dramatic than it looks, he was counterposing a socialism based on abstract internationalism, which he called "Bolshevism", to one rooted in a particular nation, which he called "Fascism". Neither term was being used in the sense that is generally accepted in our day.

Not Marx but Bakunin

Other seeming endorsements of fascism usually turn out to mean something else. In 1924 MacDiarmid reviewed *James Connolly* by the Irish writer Desmond Ryan, together with a book on Marx and Bakunin. He quoted Æ, who had said that Connolly's attempts to rationalise his nationalism and socialism were not convincing, MacDiarmid suggested that Russell was thinking of the older, internationalist, type of socialism, and had failed to observe the reorientation of the socialist movement. In Scotland former Marxists, previously concerned only with economic change, had become ardent Home Rulers.

Since the Russian Revolution, he suggested, Marx had been superseded within European socialism by Bakunin, who had favoured federalism. "And however opposed Marxian Socialism and Nationalism may seem to be, Bakunin's 'Anarchy' with its insistence on the necessity for the destruction of all centralised States ... offers easy means of reconciliation."[50] He cited a passage from Gorgolini, which opposed any socialism or pacifism without patriotism and concluded, "Fascism, then, may be regarded as a form of reaction against Marxism: but it can only succeed for a while – Italian Socialism on the new basis not of Marx but of Bakunin will eventually overcome it."[51] This was followed by a quote from Ramsay MacDonald, on the Scottish sense of national identity.

He had quoted Connolly, Gorgolini and MacDonald, and called in aid fascism, anarchism, and the Scottish socialist tradition. And "nationalism", "Home Rule" and "federalism" were used as synonymous terms. He understood "fascism" as meaning a synthesis of socialism and nationalism and he did not distinguish it from the very different syntheses of James Connolly and Ramsay MacDonald. He was using "fascism" to express his own ideas, but he had no consistent view of what it actually was.

A few years later he reviewed John Gawsworth's *Apes Japes and Hitlerism,* which was a defence of Wyndham Lewis and his book, *Hitler*. MacDiarmid praised Lewis as "... a splendid protagonist of the free man" and quoted his description of Hitler:

> *... resolved, with that admirable tenacity, hardihood, and intellectual acumen of the Teuton. Not to take their politics second-hand, not to also drift, but to seize the bull of finance by the horns....*[52]

He commented, "Can there be any better description than the passage I have italicised of what ought to be the spirit of the Scottish Movement ... ?"[53] He was praising the apparent audacity of the German leader not endorsing Nazi ideology, but he provoked a letter from W. Aitken (not MacDiarmid's friend W. R. Aitken), who asked:

> ... do Mr. Grieve's Communism, Douglasism and Hitlerism consist, not in any devotion to the principles involved, but to a merely objective admiration for anything which claims to oppose the existing order?"[54]

MacDiarmid replied that, in quoting Lewis on Hitler, he had not meant to endorse the passage, but to support the,

> ... vital force ... resourcefulness and colour which attracts me in Hitler as, say, against the ... horrible local preacherism, writ large, of Ramsay MacDonald. ... I personally prefer any manifest tendency whatever to mere opportunism and sitting on the fence ... We must oppose every attempt at finality – every system that seeks to establish a closed order – every theory that threatens to put an end to the restless ever-changing spirit of mankind; and as Dostoevski pointed out long ago every human organisation sooner or later aims at that.[55]

Aitken was right, much of what MacDiarmid wrote about fascism was motivated by his support for "anything which claims to oppose the existing order." In this spirit he claimed to approve of the Scottish Fascist Democratic Party which wanted to deprive Scottish Catholics of citizenship and also "any policy (and the better the more violent) the Catholics adopt to counter it." Anything that would, "shake the masses of our people out of their indifferentism will be to the good. I am out for a fight, and I do not care very much what means might prove useful to that end."[56] In fact he welcomed immigration from Ireland and he would never have supported persecution of Irish Catholics in Scotland.

Submission to the Roman Catholic Church

MacDiarmid is not usually thought of as a Catholic writer, but this is an important line of enquiry. In 1977 Nancy K. Gish asked him about some of his neo-Catholic poems and sonnets.[57] He replied: "... that was a sort of spin off of the interest I had then in Maurras, ... And that didn't last long. But if I had been attracted to any form of Christianity, it would certainly have been the Roman Catholic Church." His Catholic phase was not as fleeting this suggests. During his army service, in a letter to George Ogilvie, he wrote about his, "... progress through the pit of atheism to Roman Catholicism (adherent not member of the Church of Rome – I doubt my faiths and doubt my doubts of my faith too subtly to take the final step ...). He added, "I shall come back and start a new neo-Catholic movement. I shall enter heart and body and soul into a new Scots Nationalist propaganda."[58]

In November 1925 H. Brown of Greenock attempted to sum up in sixteen points the ideas to be found in MacDiarmid's *Contemporary Scottish Studies*. He suggested, that what the articles were saying was that Scottish culture and psychology were distinct from those of England. That Scottish culture had developed out of the ethnic and linguistic groups which had occupied Scottish soil in the past. That the psychology of the Scots was fundamentally Celtic, but it was now impracticable to resurrect Gaelic as the vernacular. Since English culture was now decadent, a Scottish Renaissance had to return to the fifteenth century, the highest point of Scottish cultural achievement. And the Scottish Renaissance was an elite group which would lead the rest of the nation in creating this new culture. MacDiarmid replied that, with the insertion of two minor amendments, Brown's points, "admirably describe my position and my programme."[59]

This was a Catholic strategy in two senses. It would take Scotland back to the point at which its culture had been "interrupted" by the Reformation. And it would situate its culture within world culture, through re-establishing it as part of Catholic Europe. A subsequent letter by Brown put an additional five points, in an attempt to get a clearer definition of the relationship between the Scottish Renaissance and Catholicism. The core of every sound culture, he suggested, was its theology. A catholic theology would, *"form the permanent living core of a world culture"*, but would have to be modified to suit the psychology of different peoples and ages. *"The supreme task of the Scottish Renaissance is to achieve an appropriate modification of catholic* [sic] *theology."* In so doing it was *"often helpful, but never necessary, and not always sufficient to make submission to the Roman Catholic Church as it now is."*[60]

MacDiarmid assented to these propositions, but pointed out that Brown had not defined "culture" and it was possible that they meant entirely different things by the word.[61] For him the issue was not about personal faith, nor about the relationship of the Church of Rome to world Christianity. It was about how Scottish culture might become part of European culture. On the issue of faith his position seems still to have been, "I doubt my faiths and doubt my doubts of my faith."

Apollonian or Faustian

The two "fascist" articles were precursors of his short book *Albyn,* published in 1927, based on an essay written for Æ's *Irish Statesman.*[62] In *Albyn* he developed and systemised a number of the arguments he had put forward in 1923, but he made no reference to fascism and he showed much more interest in France than in Italy or Germany. He claimed that the Scottish Renaissance would, in retrospect, be seen to have had a common genesis with "other phenomena of recrudescent nationalism all over Europe and to have shared to the full in the wave of Catholic revivalism which accompanied them."[63]

The most important right-wing influence on the book was Oswald Spengler, who is best known for his cyclical theory of historical development, in which human civilisations go through an organic process of growth, full flowering, and decline. Marnie Hughes Warrington suggests that the timing of Spengler's best known book had an important impact on how it was interpreted.

> *The Decline of the West* gave voice to the public suspicion that the collapse of Germany between 1918 and 1923 was a symptom of a wider malaise. In the twentieth century people lost faith in the ideas of historical progress. Rather they saw the conflicts of their own time as evidence of decline. Spengler confirmed their vision of the world.[64]

This pessimism led a number of European fascist and extreme right wing movements to believe that the degeneration of western civilisation could only be reversed by the leadership of a superman, at the head of a militarised nation. But MacDiarmid interpreted Spengler in the opposite way. In his "Theory of Scots Letters" of 1923, he wrote, "Spengler is no pessimist: to translate the title of his book *The Downfall of the Western World,* is to suggest a false idea of it. The idea he seeks to convey is rather 'fulfilment' – the end of one civilisation and the beginning of another – the emergence of a new order."[65] He went on:

> Of the many antithesis of which Herr Spengler builds up his thesis ... that which predominates ... is the distinction he draws between the 'Apollonian' or classical and the 'Faustian' or modern type. The Apollonian type is dogmatic, unquestioning, instinctive having no concept of infinity – in short your average Englishman or German – and the Faustian mind, on the contrary is dominated by the conception of infinity, of the unattainable,

and hence is ever questioning, never satisfied, rationalistic in religion and politics, romantic in art and literature – a perfect expression of the Scots race.[66]

"Apollonian" or "Apollinian" is a term used by Spengler to refer to an existence which, "... lacks all idea of an inner development and therefore all real history, inward and outward." By "Faustian" he meant an existence which, "... *is led* by a deep consciousness and introspection of the ego, and a resolutely personal culture evidenced in memoirs, reflections, retrospects and prospects and conscience."[67] The words can be understood as contrasting terms for the Classical and the Gothic cultures, particularly their architectural styles.

Spengler considered the Apollinian and the Faustian, together with the Magian (Arab) cultures, to be part of a tripartite division. But MacDiarmid made no reference to the Magian and he categorised German culture as Apollinian, whereas for Spengler it was Faustian. But MacDiarmid's interpretation was the well spring of his optimism. If the Apollinian culture of England was exhausted, space was being created into which a revived Scottish culture could erupt. As he explained in *Contemporary Scottish Studies,* Spengler's theories had led him to,

> ... see a potentially-creative interrelationship between such ostensibly unrelated phenomena as the emergence of the 'Glasgow Group' of Socialist M.P.'s; the intensification of the Scottish Home Rule movement; the growth of Scottish Catholicism; and the movement for the revival of Braid Scots. As soon as I began to interest myself in the possibilities of a Scottish Renaissance I found that I was by no means alone in doing so. The matter was definitely 'in the air'.[68]

Albyn was the political manifesto that accompanied his cultural manifesto of *Contemporary Scottish Studies.* In both books he identified five groupings within contemporary Scotland that were converging, to bring about a reflorescence of the country's national life. They were:

1. The Scottish Renaissance, which was recreating an authentic national culture.
2. The "Clyde Rebels" who were showing signs of returning to the Home Rule ideas of Keir Hardie.
3. The Scottish national movement, which meant the Scottish Home Rule Association and the Scots National League, who were soon to be united as the National Party of Scotland.

4. The Crofters, who were reviving the Highland land agitation of the 1880s.
5. Irish immigration, which had the potential to re-Celticise Scotland, to counter Scottish Calvinism, and to link Scotland with Catholic Europe.

A Gaelic Programme

Albyn was a phase in his move back to the left but although some of his writings seem, on the surface, to be anti-Communist, the seeds of his conversion can be discerned. In grappling with the problem of how to respond to the Soviet Union he, initially, adopted an apparently right-wing stance, in March 1928, he recommended Wyndham Lewis's periodical *The Enemy*,

> He points especially to the general hatred of intellect – the increasing communism which detests all that makes one man or race distinctive and sets up comparative values. ... we learn that 'mind' is of all things what Bolshevism is concerned to deny and prohibit".[69]

He believed that the Soviet state was suppressing the intelligentsia, but he never shared the outright loathing of the Bolshevik revolution expressed by some other *New Age* writers. In his *Neo-Gaelic Economics* of February 1928, he quoted from Robert Graves, who had said that the "future of English prosody" depended on the outcome of class antagonism. "A Red victory would bring with it ... a revival of the native prosody in a fairly pure form ... ."[70] MacDiarmid commented, "Russian post-revolution literature and language fully substantiates Graves's contention."[71] This was an early sign of a more positive attitude towards the USSR.

In July 1928 he wrote to Compton Mackenzie, saying that he was "beating up the Scottish Socialist Movement" by arguing that a "Gaelic Commonwealth" was "more in keeping with our national genius" than a "Workers' Commonwealth."[72] *The Gaelic Commonwealth* was the title of a book by Fr. William Ferris, a Catholic chaplain to the Irish Free State Army,[73] he was a conservative opponent of parliamentary democracy. who proposed a decentralised monarchical system, based on the political structures of Celtic Ireland. MacDiarmid wrote, "Mr. Ferris has dug down to bed-rock principle in every detail and has furnished a Gaelic programme in salient contrast in every respect to the other programmes at present applied or advocated either in Ireland or Scotland..."[74]

He agreed with Ferris that western parliamentary systems had failed and that representative government was, "merely a species of bloodless warfare in which the strongest and more numerous side always wins … ".[75] This was in line with his anti-democratic rhetoric of the time, but he also praised the book's arguments for social justice, which were derived from Papal teachings against usury and wage slavery.

In February 1929 he wrote about the, "danger of the Socialist championship of class – as against the Nationalist espousal of the interests of the whole people," and he recommended Social Credit as a replacement for the socialist "spirit of class antagonism."[76] In January 1930 he told Oliver St. John Gogarty that he had been an active socialist but, "my views have changed very considerably and on the whole I think I can now best be described as a 'crusted old Tory'."[77] In *Scottish Scene,* published in 1934 but written earlier, he argued that Social Credit was an alternative to both fascism and communism.[78]

The Essence of Platonism

The title of his 1931 collection, *First Hymn to Lenin*, is deceptive. Only the title poem and "Seamless Garment" refer to Lenin. In a review of the *First Hymn*, written for the Unicorn Press under the pseudonym "James McLaren", MacDiarmid said:

> … in the final stanza it rises into a whole-hearted espousal of Leninism which … will only be surprising to those who allow their own political prejudices to make them imagine that he is expressly subscribing to Russian Sovietism instead of voicing in memorable fashion the essence of Platonism.[79]

By "Platonism" he meant that Lenin was a "philosopher ruler", whose understanding of the fundamental truths of human existence enabled him, (as a classic study of Plato put it), to " transfer the perfect law, of which he has the vision, into the characters and institutions of men, like a great artist taking human nature as he finds it and moulding it in the light of his own high conception.…[80] "Platonism" also referred to a philosophical principle, Plato maintained that the appearances of the material world, as perceived by the senses, are only shadows of reality. It is the principles behind these appearances, the "forms" which are real, and they are not material but ideal. In the *Republic* Plato depicted Socrates arguing that only philosophers can distinguish between the facile, fleeting, impressions of the senses and the eternal realities which lie behind them, so that only they are able to rule with justice.

In *Lucky Poet* MacDiarmid quoted from Orage's review of the *First Hymn*:

> The "First Hymn to Lenin" has the quiet magnificence of homage rendered freely by one man to another; it approaches the spirit of the Pindaric odes. In the "Seamless Garment," ... MacDiarmid is affectionately "explaining" Lenin much in the same way as Ezra Pound wrote of Jesus in his "Ballade of the Goodly Fere."[81]

Tim Redman explains the parallel with Ezra Pound,

> Both Lenin and Mussolini were Poundian heroes. Both were men who understood the specific historical situation existing in their countries and both were decisive enough to turn that understanding to account. Both were artists of a new kind of art form ... halfway between thought and political action.[82]

In MacDiarmid's poem Lenin symbolised those leaders whose powerful intellects and personalities enabled them change human existence. But his approval of Lenin as a philosopher ruler was not yet an endorsement of Marxist ideology.

A Group who do not Look Like a Group

In the mid-1920s MacDiarmid was still the utopian he had been as a young ILP socialist in Edinburgh. Through a restless grappling with new ideas he was continually stretching towards what was more complete and perfect, in his search for a strategy that could free Scotland from political subordination and cultural mediocrity. In the course of this, he became interested in fascism, but by the time he came write *Albyn* he had realised that it did not meet his purpose. The *First Hymn* was written when he was just beginning to explore another idea, that the Soviet Union had opened up new possibilities for humanity, and therefore for Scotland.

Trying to fit MacDiarmid into a fascist framework misses the point. In the 1920s, he was influenced by right wing ideas, but not by fascist ones. He was influenced by the writers Orwell categorised as a "group," despite the fact that they "do not look like a group"[83] They included "Joyce, Eliot, Pound, Lawrence, Wyndham Lewis, Aldous Huxley, Lytton Stratchey." Orwell identified their unifying characteristic as pessimism. "All of them are temperamentally hostile to the notion of 'progress'; it is felt that progress not only doesn't happen but ought not to happen."[84]

Many writers of the 1920s experienced the post-war world as a wasteland and some, usually temporarily, saw fascism as a way to rescue western civilization from decadence. But MacDiarmid was not one of them, he was optimistic because he saw the decline of the west as an opportunity for Scotland to emerge from stagnation and to reassume its status as an independent European nation. This optimism meant that he remained a utopian and was always much more likely to become a Communist than a fascist. Utopianism was also the reason for his adoption of Major Douglas's Social Credit.

Notes

1. *Complete Poems op. cit.* p. 94.
2. *cf.* Henry Maitles, "Fascism in the 1930s: The West of Scotland experience," *Journal of the Scottish Labour History Society*, No. 27, 1992, pp. 7–22.
3. *The Scottish Worker*, 10 May 1926.
4. See the description by David Howell in *British Workers and the Independent Labour Party,* Manchester University Press, 1983, p. 2.
5. Alan Bold (ed.) *The Letters of Hugh MacDiarmid*, University of Georgia Press, 1984, p. 5.
6. GDH Cole, *Guild Socialism,* London, The Fabian Society, 1920, p. 4.
7. *Letters,* p. 11.
8. *Letters,* p. 4.
9. See Bob Holton, *British Syndicalism, 1900–1914. Myths and Realities,* London, Pluto Press, 1976, pp. 78–81.
10. *Letters,* p. 879.
11. Alan Riach *(ed.), Hugh MacDiarmid. Selected Prose*, Manchester, Carcarnet, 1992, pp. 203–4.
12. William W. Craik, *The Central Labour College, 109–29. A Chapter in the History of Working-class Education, London, Lawrence & Wishart, 1964, p. 90.*
13. See Bob Holton, *British Syndicalism 1900–1914. Myths and Realities,* London, Pluto, 1976, pp. 168–70.
14. Hywel Francis and David Smith, *The Fed. A History of the South Wales Miners' in the Twentieth Century,* London, Lawrence & Wishart, 1980, p. 10.
15. Wallace Martin, *The New Age Under Orage*, Manchester University Press & New York, Barnes & Noble, 1967, p. 198.
16. Alan Bold. *MacDiarmid. Christopher Murray Grieve. A Critical Biography,* London, John Murray, 1988, pp. 146–7.
17. Hamish Henderson, *The Armstrong Nose,* Edinburgh, Polygon, 1996, p. 167.
18. *Raucle Tongue, The III,* p. 596.
19. *Ibid.,* p. 596.
20. *The Armstrong Nose,* p. 170.
21. Denis Mack Smith, "A Prehistory of Fascism" in A. William Salamone (ed.) *Italy From the Risorgimento to Fascism*, Newton Abbot, David & Charles, 1971, pp. 104–5.
22. *The Armstrong Nose,* p. 166.

23. Pietro Gorgolini, *The Fascist Movement in Italian Life*, Edited with Introduction by M. D. Petre, London, T. Fisher Unwin Ltd., 1923. Odon Por, *Fascism*, Translated by Emily Townshend, [American edition], New York, A. Knopf, 1923.

24. *A Survey of Fascism the Year Book of the International Centre for Fascist Studies*, Vol. 1, London, Ernest Benn, 1928, p. 236.

25. *Ibid.*, p. 149.

26. *Fascism;* p. 152.

27. *Ibid., op cit* p. 9.

28. *Ibid.*, pp. 185–6.

29. *The Irish Statesman* 15 September 1923.

30. *The Glasgow Herald* 17th April 1923.

31. *The Fascist Movement in Italian Life*, p. 136.

32. *Ibid.*, p. 91.

33. *The Scottish Nation* September 4th 1923, quoting Por, *op. cit*, pp. 3 & 5–6. **N. B.** This review was published over the initials "T. S. E." and has not previously been identified as by MacDiarmid, I am grateful to Owen Dudley Edwards, John Manson and Alan Riach for supporting my attribution. See the appendix for the full text.

34. *Pictish Review*, April 1928.

35. *The Free Man* April 16th 1932.

36. The full text can be found in Margery Palmer McCulloch (ed.) *Modernism and Nationalism: Literature and Society in Scotland 1918–1939, Source Documents for the Scottish Renaissance*, Glasgow, The Association for Scottish Literary Studies, 2004, pp. 349–50.

37. *The Free Man*, August 26th. Also in *Modernism and Nationalism*, p. 351.

38. *Raucle Tongue, The I, op. cit.*, p. 83.

39. *cf.* Iain Fraser Grigor, *Highland Resistance. The Radical Tradition in the Scottish North* Edinburgh & London, Mainstream, 2000, pp. 203–5, Leah Leneman, *Land Fit for Heroes? Land Settlement in Scotland After World War I*, Aberdeen University Press, 1989, pp. 117–125.

40. *Raucle Tongue, The I*, p. 210.

41. *Ibid.*, p. 85, italics in original.

42. *Ibid.*, p. 84.

43. "The Doctrine of Fascism" in Adrian Lyttleton (ed.) *Italian Fascisms from Pareto to Gentile*, Cape, London, 1973, p. 43.

44. *Raucle Tongue, The I*, p. 86.

45. *The Fascist Movement in Italian Life*, pp. 16–17.

46. *Raucle Tongue, The I*, p. 86.

47. *The Fascist Movement in Italian Life*, p. 200.

48. *Selected Prose*, p. 36.

49. *Raucle Tongue, The I*, pp. 103–4.

50. *Ibid.*, p. 210.

51. *Ibid.*, p. 209.

52. *The Free Man*, July 1932, italics in the original.

53. *Ibid.*

54. *The Free Man* August 13th 1932.

55. *The Free Man* September 3rd 1932.

56. *The Free Man*, May 26th 1933.

57. *Raucle Tongue, The III*, p. 579.

58. *Letters*, p. 13.

59. *Contemporary Scottish Studies*, pp. 231–2.

60. *Ibid.*, p. 243. Italics in original.

61. *Ibid.,* p. 258–9.
62. 16th July 1926.
63. *Albyn,* p. 1.
64. Marnie Hughes Warrington, *Fifty Key Thinkers on History,* London & New York, Routledge, 2000, p. 288.
65. *Selected Prose, op. cit.* p. 26. The title he used suggests that he read the German version.
66. *Ibid.,* p. 27.
67. Oswald Spengler, *The Decline of the West,* Authorised translation with notes by Charles Francis Atkinson, New York, Alfred A. Knopf, Vol. 1, 1927, p. 183.
68. p. 95.
69. *Raucle Tongue, The II,* p. 46.
70. *Ibid.,* p. 65.
71. *Ibid.*
72. *New Selected Letters,* p. 33.
73. William Ferris, *The Gaelic Commonwealth: Being the Political and Economic Programme for the Irish Progressive Party.* Dublin: Talbot Press, 1923.
74. *The Scottish Nation* October 9th 1923.
75. *Ibid.*
76. *Raucle Tongue, The II,* p. 77.
77. *Letters,* p. 383.
78. Lewis Grassic Gibbon & Hugh MacDiarmid (eds.) *Scottish Scene,* London, Hutchinson & Co., 1934. p. 126.
79. University of Delaware MS225, Box 1, Folder 5. I am grateful to the University of Delaware Library for supplying copies of a typescript and of the holographic original.
80. G. R. Bénson, (ed.) Richard Lewis Nettleship *Lectures on the Republic of Plato,* London, MacMillan, 1910, pp. 210–11.
81. *Hugh MacDiarmid Lucky Poet,* Manchester, Carcarnet, 1994 edited by Alan Riach. p. 76.
82. Tim Redman, *Ezra Pound and Italian Fascism,* Cambridge University Press, 1991, p. 109.
83. *Inside the Whale and Other Essays,* Penguin, Harmondsworth, 1957, p. 25.
84. *Ibid.,* p. 26.

2

Green

MacDiarmid and Social Credit

The end of international finance –
Consciously or unconsciously, it matters not –
Is universal degradation and slavery,
A foul circumspection of the human lot.

But the Puritan asceticism is gone for ever
Which made the working-masses ashamed
Of their poverty as of a crime
For which they were in some way to be blamed.

And a sense of power and set resolve
Is abroad to shatter the shackles at last
And make all usury, poverty, and needless toil
Memories of an obscene incredible past.

("The End of Usury" from *Second Hymn to Lenin*.)[1]

Social Credit is the least understood aspect of MacDiarmid's politics and yet it was his most enduring political commitment. It linked him with a number of thinkers and movements who were on the right of the political spectrum, but also with the utopian socialism of his youth. It was a critique of the monetary system and a plan for economic reform which was developed in the 1920s by Major Clifford Hugh Douglas, a retired army engineer. Its greatest influence was between 1931 and 1939, after the Wall Street Crash and the abandonment of the Gold Standard.

Major Douglas's system assumed that economic depression was caused by an avoidable shortage of credit. As Andrew Marr explains,

> … he thought that as wealth grew through technological advance, it should simply be divided each year among everyone, whether they worked or not, and passed to them as their share of the national dividend. Power would be removed from the Bank of England because 'the Credit of a community belongs to the community as

a whole'. Eventually as societies grew richer through technical progress unemployment would disappear and people would have to work far less: the 'leisure society' would be born.[2]

Douglas' ideas bore some resemblance to JA Hobson's underconsumptionist economic theory, which held that lack of purchasing power led to economic depression, and also to the credit and monetary reform advocates Silvio Gesell and Frederick Soddy. All of them explained the economic problems of the capitalist system as consequences of the financial system, not as defects of the productive sector.

Douglas's proposals were taken up by the editor of *The New Age,* Alfred Richard Orage, and Social Credit appealed to many in the literary and artistic world. Ezra Pound wrote Social Credit poetry and polemics, Storm Jameson and Eimar O'Duffy wrote Social Credit novels and TS Eliot was a sympathiser. The writers William MacLellan, Compton Mackenzie, Edwin Muir and Denis Ireland were sympathetic, as were the artists William McCance and Augustus John, (who painted a portrait of Douglas).

A Vital Fallacy

A Scottish supporter, "H.M.M." (H. M. Murray),[3] wrote a biographical sketch of Major Douglas. As Chief Engineer and Manager of the Westinghouse Company in India in the 1910s he had discovered potential water power, but had been frustrated by the lack of finance to develop it. During the First World War he worked on cost accounting at the Royal Aircraft Factory at Farnborough, where he noticed that the total costs of production, in the form of machinery and raw materials, always exceeded the amount paid out in wages, salaries and dividends.

His study of 100 large firms showed that this was a common phenomenon and Douglas concluded that the wealth being distributed to society was never enough to purchase all the goods produced by industry. The Controller-General of India had told him that "silver and gold have nothing to do with the situation; it nearly entirely depends on credit"[4]. He realised that production was financed by credit issued by the banks and not by tangible assets such as gold. Douglas, who had no qualifications as an economist, came to believe that in issuing credit the banks were, in effect, creating money out of thin air and that their monopoly of credit prevented the distribution of sufficient purchasing power to the general population.

Social Credit was based on a number of linked ideas:

- All credit values derive from the community and are the product of labour expended in the past as well as in the present.

- The rate at which goods are produced depends on the "cultural inheritance of the community". This refers to the advances in science, skills and understanding made by people in the past, which have made possible the machines, tools and processes which enhance productivity in the present.
- The financial system derives "all financial values from credit which takes all these factors into account". Credit issue and pricing are the "positive and negative aspects of the function which controls the economic life of the community, and so controls the community itself".
- Despite this "the community does not control credit-issue or price-making at present."
- The prices charged for commodities include two sets of costs, "A" items, which are payments made to individuals in the form of wages, salaries and dividends and "B" items", payments made to other organisations for raw materials, bank charges and other external costs. There is a chronic deficiency in purchasing power because "A" is always less than "A+B".
- Credit is created by the banks to finance production and to enable consumers to purchase the goods which have been produced. In doing this the banks create new money, since deposits made by savers represent only a tiny fraction of the value of the money issued. This credit, which is essential to overcome the deficiency in purchasing power, is then regarded as a debt to the banks.
- This system concentrates ownership and control in the hands of financiers and gives them unaccountable power, which undermines democracy.[5]

MacDiarmid quoted a succinct explanation of the Major's central thesis:

... under present conditions the purchasing power in the hands of the community is chronically insufficient to buy the whole product of industry. This is because the money required to finance capital production, and created by the banks for that purpose, is regarded as borrowed from them, and therefore, in order that it may be repaid, is charged into the price of the consumer's goods. It is a vital fallacy to treat new money thus created by the banks as a repayable loan without crediting the community, on the strength of whose resources the money was created, with the value of the resulting new capital resources. This has given rise to a defective system of national loan accountancy, resulting in the reduction of the community to a condition of perpetual scarcity, and bringing them face to face with the alternative of widespread unemployment of men and machines, as at present, or of international complications arising from the struggle for foreign markets.[6]

According to H. M. Murray, if all the costs of production were traced back to their original source they would be seen to be payments made for goods, services and etc. He argued that, although it might seem that the community always has sufficient money to buy what is produced, "the items appearing in costs today represent payments made over a long period of time ... but to be effective as purchasing power *now* ... every penny of those payments would have had to be saved." But, "most of the money was spent as it was received ... and no longer exists as purchasing power ...[7].

Major Douglas and his followers were convinced that a vast store of purchasing power was locked up by the banks and denied as spending to consumers. The state, they said, should issue credits up to the value of all the goods produced and distribute these as a just wage, as subsidies to ensure just prices and as a national dividend paid to every citizen. This would create a society of abundance, enjoyment of which would be a right of citizenship and not a reward for effort. They had a vision of a world which would provide everyone with a basic income without demanding irksome toil.

They did not, however, have a single explanation of why the situation described by the Major had come about. For some it was a previously unrecognised "mathematical fallacy in accounting"[8] while for others it was due to secret manipulation by "the financiers" who were, "aided by their friends the Big Business monopolists and armament-makers."[9] A number of them, including Douglas, came to the conclusion that it was the result of a Jewish conspiracy.

Every Monetary Heretic

The Major provoked a response from qualified economists, including two young left wing academics, the future Labour leader Hugh Gaitskell and his friend Evan Durbin. Their arguments against Douglas helped them to shape the economic policies of the post-1945 Labour Government.[10] Gaitskell commented:

> ... every monetary heretic offers a single complete solution.... There is to be no painful waiting, no lowering of standards, no difficult compromises ... the heretic is able to enlist support just because he is not an expert ... He is a plain practical man, proving to other plain practical men that the mysteries which these exalted intellects are alone suffered to understand are matters which can be made perfectly intelligible to the rest of the community.[11]

Gaitskell and Durbin criticised the "A + B theorem", which seemed to be a be a way of measuring how much credit was likely to be issued. A Labour Party pamphlet claimed that Douglas's "Plan for Scotland" depended on multiple counting of the same values and that he had given two different interpretations of A+B, neither of which sustained his argument.[12] It was alleged that the Major's estimate of Scotland's wealth included the capital value of all assets, including the productive capacity of individuals. These were only consumed at the rate of their depreciation, and consumers usually had enough purchasing power to pay for them. If purchasing power were to be distributed at the value proposed, instead of at the rate of depreciation, this would be used to purchase consumer goods and would result in "a gigantic inflation."[13] A similar critique was made by the Communist Party theoretician Maurice Dobb.[14] Douglas defended himself on the basis that he had only claimed that the "rate of flow" of A and B items created a deficiency in credit, not that there was a gap at every point in the process.

Pressed by John MacLeod, of the Scottish Workers Educational Association, H. M. Murray wrote, "… the logic of the A+B business is perfectly watertight. If the people engaged in every single business cannot, with their incomes … buy all they produce – as it is universally agreed they cannot, it follows inexorably that the people in all businesses cannot, with their joint incomes, buy all they jointly produce."[15] Advocates of Social Credit often retreated to general claims of this kind, when attempts were made to pin down what, exactly, was meant by the "A + B" formula.

The Major had challenged, probably unknowingly, "Say's Law of Markets", proposed by the eighteenth century French economist Jean-Baptiste Say. He had argued that supply creates its own demand and G. D. H. Cole cited this law in arguing that Douglas was mistaken when he claimed that a huge amount of purchasing power was being denied to the community by the banks. There were occasional "epidemic occurrences of deficiency of purchasing power," but there was no "endemic deficiency" because supply and demand would balance out over time.[16] But J. M. Keynes included Douglas in his list of thinkers who had recognised the error in Say's Law, and that supply and demand do not automatically balance out. They had understood that lack of purchasing power generated economic depressions like that of 1931 however, Keynes conceded, the A + B theorem had created "much mere mystification."[17]

C.B. MacPherson emphasised that Douglas had a "broader case" for Social Credit. This was based on the "technological heritage" – improvements in productive techniques from which the banks benefited through their control of credit. These factors led Douglas to conclude that financiers were manipulating the system in their own interests and that "the issuance of social credit up to the limit of the utmost potential productivity, could bring about plenty and leisure for all without disturbing any except the financiers' interests".[18] Expressed in this way, the utopian aims of Social Credit are clear, but this was obscured by the debate about economic theory.

The Master Idea

MacDiarmid did not attempt to defend the A + B theorem, he simply dismissed such criticisms as the "parrot-cries of nit-wits."[19] He claimed that Social Credit was based on "a mathematical demonstration which has not been and cannot be refuted."[20] In *Scottish Scene* he wove it into the strategy he had developed in *Albyn*:

> ... the Programme of Scotland is (1) to recover and ensue the essence of its own genius ... (2) to reduce England from its Ascendancy internally, imperially and internationally to its own proper national condition (3) to reaffiliate with Europe, and recognise our duty as the Western Frontier of Europe – a duty that includes not only the realisation of Douglasism and its fullest implications ... but also ... [as] a corrective and complement of the great Russian Experiment which has temporarily unbalanced Europe.[21]

He first mentioned Douglas in his introduction to *Contemporary Scottish Studies*, in which he listed him as one of the people to be discussed at a future date,[22] and he set out the case he was to argue for another fifty years. The Major had " 'got to the bottom of economics', and shown the way to the Workless State" He saw Douglas's ideas as a counterweight to Scottish "commercial Calvinism with its hideous doctrine of the 'need to work,' 'the necessity of drudgery' and its devices of thrift and the whole tortuous paraphernalia of modern capitalism ..."[23] It was, he said, the "master idea" he had been looking for when the Scottish national movement began. As he put it in *Scottish Scene*, "Scottish genius has been disproportionately embodied in engineering on the one hand and economics on the other ... Douglas fused and transcended these two in an unmistakable fashion....[24]

In a letter to Neil Gunn of September 1931 he said he was "moving actively in the inner circle of the Douglas School – seeing Orage himself and others. *The New Age* forecasts are all coming true – but the real crisis won't be for a year or two."[25] A couple of weeks later he told

Gunn that he had, "made arrangements with Douglas and Orage ... with regard to my taking over all the essential literature of the anti-banks movement" he had plans to "break through the grotesque position that has hitherto kept Douglasism out of American journalism" and also to "develop very quickly the existing position in regard to the New Economics in Canada and Australia".[26]

In March 1932 he was confident of an imminent breakthrough, "Douglas Social Credit Associations are multiplying rapidly. It is only a question of a little time now before the issue forces itself into the open. The question, however is whether it will do so speedily enough to avert a general economic smash-up with disastrous consequences for humanity at large".[27] Frustrated by the refusal of his colleagues on the Unicorn Press in London to publish the Major's books, he personally published *Warning Democracy* in 1931.[28]

MacDiarmid was active in the Social Credit movement only for a short period in the 1930s, but he continued to propagate its ideas for the rest of his life. In 1947, when Scottish Social Credit had been reduced to a handful of supporters, he was still optimistic about the emergence of a Social Credit Party, which would "update and implement" the Major's ideas.[29] In 1951, in "The Human Use of Human Beings the Challenge of Social Credit,"[30] he wrote about the implications of computer technology, and the possibilities it offered, of a society of abundance. In 1953 he supported a judicial enquiry into the application of Douglas's ideas to Scotland.[31] In 1956, a few months before he rejoined the Communist Party, he broadcast about Douglas's ideas on the Northern English region of the BBC.[32] And in 1959 he contributed an article to the *Partick East Social Credit Courier,* an election broadsheet issued by his friend William MacLellan, who was the Social Credit election agent for the municipal election.

The Kindred

In the 1920s Douglas tried to promote his ideas by influencing elite opinion, but with little success. In 1922 Orage retreated to France to become a disciple of the esoteric teacher Gurdjieff, when he returned to London in 1930 the economic crisis was reviving interest in Douglas's proposals. In this period, a number of other groups and individuals took up the cause. So it is best to look at the Social Credit movement as a series of loosely linked episodes.

The Major set up the Social Credit Secretariat in 1933, to expound his scheme. Orage initiated the Chandos Group, a circle of artists, writers and churchmen interested in the Major's ideas. There also was "Christendom" an Anglo-Catholic group led by Maurice Reckitt, which included prominent Christian Socialists like R. H. Tawney, George Lansbury, and Charles Gore. Another Christian proponent of Social Credit was Hewlett Johnson, later to become well known as the fellow-travelling "Red Dean" of Canterbury (by which time he had repudiated his Douglasite views). The Marquis of Tavistock, later Duke of Bedford, created the National Credit Association and issued a stream of Social Credit pamphlets. During the Second World War he was associated with extreme right wing anti-war groups.

Despite Douglas's opposition to party political activity, in 1935 a "Social Credit Party" was established in the Canadian province of Alberta by William Aberhart, a popular radio preacher. It won a landslide election victory in the provincial elections. The party's manifesto had proposed a monthly dividend of $25, paid to every citizen, but instead it offered an "Alberta Prosperity Certificate", a dollar bill, on which a stamp worth either one or two cents had to be stuck each week if it was to retain its value. This was intended to stimulate the economy by increasing the velocity of money, but Major Douglas denounced the policy as a crude implementation of the ideas of the German currency reformer, Silvio Gesell.[33] In any case, the legislation was blocked at federal level. Despite this setback Social Credit parties on the Aberhart model were established in other Canadian provinces and also in Australia and New Zealand.

The most visible group in Britain was a uniformed political movement known as the Green Shirts. It was led by John Hargrave, a journalist, novelist, artist, lexicographer, psychic healer and inventor. As "White Fox" he had written a book, *Lonecraft,* which influenced the Boy Scout movement. After the First World War, he led an anti-militarist break-away from the Scouts called "The Kindred of the Kibbo Kift". It engaged in rambling, camping and semi-mystical rituals and has been called, "the only genuinely English national movement of modern times."[34] In 1927 the Kibbo Kift was transformed into the Green Shirts for Social Credit, a uniformed movement which took the Social Credit cause onto the streets, where it clashed with both the Communists the Blackshirts.[35]

Plan for Scotland

Scottish Social Credit can be traced back to the Guild Socialists of Clydeside. John L. Finlay notes that the Glasgow and Paisley branches of the National Guilds League seceded when that body came out against Social Credit,[36] one of the Glasgow Guildsmen was H. M. Murray, who became a member of the National Party of Scotland. He "was the only writer on Social Credit to whom Douglas awarded his imprimatur."[37]

MacDiarmid always claimed that Douglas was a Scot although, in fact, he was born in Stockport. But the Major did feel sufficiently Scottish to sanction the wearing of Douglas tartan facings on the uniform of the Green Shirts[38] and, in retirement, he made his home in Perthshire. MacDiarmid persuaded him to become a member of the National Party of Scotland and, in a message for the founding of the Party, Douglas said that nationalism, "derives from within us as the trees grow from the seed." He denounced internationalism as an "impostor" which in its modern form was, "an effort to impose a ... suspect culture by control of economic resources through hidden finance."[39]

In his "Plan for Scotland", of 1932 Douglas supported small scale administration and Scottish self government:

> ... there is a definite policy being pursued to retain this power of economic government ... to make the problem always bigger and bigger. First of all see that you cannot settle it in your own village, then you cannot settle it in your own county, nor in your own country, and finally, that nothing can be done in the matter, except by world agreement. If any of you have any faith in ... world agreement ... your faith greatly transcends mine.... if there were no other reason I should be a supporter of Scottish Home Rule because it limits the problem.[40]

The Plan was published in the Glasgow *Evening Times* of 11 March and launched at a rally in the St. Andrews Hall. It proposed a dividend of £300 a year to be issued to every Scottish family. The total value of all Scotland's capital assets was to be determined and a "price value of the Scottish capital account" obtained. Financial credit to an equivalent amount would then be created by a Scottish treasury and the national dividend would initially be calculated at 1% of the capital sum. There would be a system of "assisted prices", speculation in stocks would be prevented, the ownership of stocks, shares or bonds by a holding company would no longer be recognised and no-one could dispose of real estate except to the government. An authoritarian note was struck by proposals to use the dividend as a means of controlling wage demands and to compel people into employment.

In 1935 a Social Credit Party of Scotland was formed. MacDiarmid, who was living in Shetland and had joined the Communist Party, was not involved. The party identified the financial system as the chief obstacle to achieving economic security for the Scottish people. Westminster government was a secondary obstacle but: "...it is not in the interests of Scotland to persist for sentimental or commercial or cowardly reasons in a Union with a foreign people which operates so thoroughly to her own moral and material detriment as the Union with England ..."[41] Since the constitution provided for a National Leader and a uniformed section it seems to have been imitative of the Green Shirts. But, despite being given a good deal of publicity in *The Free Man* newspaper, it did not survive for long. A less flamboyant organisation was the Glasgow Social Credit Club, which took a stand at the Empire Exhibition in Bellahouston Park in 1938 and issued a journal called *Abundance*. MacDiarmid was probably referring to this group when he forecast, in 1947, that there would soon be a Scotland-wide Social Credit Party.

Hole-Pickers and Sharp-Shooters

Social Credit had a receptive audience in the National Party of Scotland and the *Scots Independent* gave MacDiarmid's friend William Bell space to explain the scheme.[42] The 1930 annual conference agreed to a resolution from the Aberdeen Branch, calling for a committee to examine Douglas's proposals. MacDiarmid was appointed convener[43] but, at the 1931 Conference, it reported that the scheme contained proposals of value to Scotland but the "time was not ripe" to make it official policy.[44]

Social Credit did overlap with a number of ideas NPS members found attractive, but it failed to convince a majority that it was a realistic policy. Even some Douglasites were said believe that it would be "unwise to confuse the issue" by adopting it as official policy.[45] They did so on the same grounds as the Major's when he repudiated political activity, governments should not ask the people "how" they wanted something done, "the people should decide *what* they want and the Government should know *how* to get it for them."[46] In other words, Social Crediters must first convert the people, then it would be necessary for the government to respond with legalisation.

In 1933 the NPS finally turned Social Credit down and an article by Nannie K. Wells helps to explain why. She praised the "hole-pickers and sharp-shooters" who had challenged orthodox economic theory. She included in this category Major Douglas and Professor Frederick Soddy, a radiochemist and Nobel laureate who had produced a critique of the money system, similar in some respects to Social Credit. He and Douglas were bitter rivals, but she classed both schemes as the "New Economics."[47] She reflected a widespread dissatisfaction with the way in which banks, credit and money appeared to produce unemployment and scarcity at a time of unparalleled technological advance But the highly abstract claims of the competing credit theorists meant that she was unable to give exclusive support to any one of them.

Organised Functions

Hugh Gaitskell was suspicious of Douglas's proposals because he thought that the monetary system was far more unpredictable and complex than the Major understood. There was a parallel with his view that the complete abolition of money would have an undemocratic outcome,

> An economy without money would have to be entirely totalitarian and militaristic in character. Everybody would have to work where they were told to, production would be directed to the smallest detail from above and the available output would have to be rationed. An economy of this kind would not be impossible; but it would probably be very wasteful and quite unnecessarily oppressive.[48]

Evan Durbin, citing Keynes and others, argued that a programme of public investment combined with control of lending by joint stock banks was a sufficient remedy.[49] He and Gaitskell believed that a Social Credit state would have to control all economic activity because the only way to avoid inflation would be to keep the amount of credit issued strictly in line with the products available. But control of the economy on this scale would give the government far too much power and would be a threat to democracy.

Their critique of Social Credit was part of their opposition to the anti-democratic ideologies of the inter-war years and their suspicions were not groundless. When he was living in London, MacDiarmid recalled that a friend challenged him.

> "What are you doing among these people? Don't you realise that they will all go religious-Fascist?' I did not realise anything of the kind, but they all did go religious-Fascist, and I still do not see why that should be so. It has certainly not happened in my case."[50]

The solution to the puzzle can be found by examining the roots of Social Credit in Guild Socialism and *The New Age*. Orage believed that the ILP had failed because it accepted the wage system and, consequently, it had to accept rent, interest and profits. State ownership would still leave the worker in bondage to the wage system; and unemployment was an integral part of that system. Political citizenship meant nothing,

... because the possessing class evolved an "active" type of citizenship and the wage-earning class evolved a "passive" type. That, in short, the maintenance of the wage system defeated the theoretical claims of the classical democrats, producing material and psychological results peculiar to a servile state.... economic methods are essential to the achievement of economic emancipation; that political methods are useless ... economic power is the substance and political power its shadow or reflection.[51]

Private capitalism must be replaced by a system of self-contained units, run by the workers on the principles of industrial democracy. The scheme combined elements of European syndicalism and British socialist traditions, especially the ideas of Robert Owen, who had advocated small, self-governing, co-operative communities.

Hillaire Belloc's book *The Servile State* had a profound impact in *The New Age* circles because it helped to crystallise their dissatisfaction with the Fabian emphasis on state ownership as a route to socialism.

They repudiated ... the belief enshrined in the policies of the Fabians, the Webbs, and the Labour programme of 1918, that it was enough to secure public control of the instruments of production and the rent, interest, and profit they produce in order to redistribute this wealth, improve the conditions of work and otherwise efficiently meet the needs of the people.... the situation which would be produced ... would turn out to be a 'servile state' in which the workers would face, instead of capitalist dominance, a vast collectivist bureaucracy ... He would still be alienated from his work, regarded as a factor of production, merely a 'hand' or 'living tool' rather than (as he should be) a partner.[52]

What then switched *The New Age* from left to right was the concept of "functionalism", which refers to the principle that the rights of a citizen should be a consequence of her function as a producer. As the Spanish thinker Ramiro de Maetzu, expressed it, "... rights ought to be granted to men or associations of men in virtue of the function they fulfil ... ".[53] This paralleled the Syndicalist and Guild Socialist concept of a citizenship rooted in the organisations of workers at the point of production.

It led Odon Por to argue that Italian Fascism fulfilled Guild Socialist ideas:

Italy is in the midst of organising the Corporative Nation-State, in which every activity will be represented in its organised aspect, with functions considered as public ones.... During the world-war, and long before there was any sign of fascism, certain writers, the "guildsmen," predicted … that the primitive class struggle would eventually transform itself into a higher and more complex struggle – that is, into a process of competition and selection of organised functions, aiming at the common good.[54]

Odon Por was a close friend of Ezra Pound and had influential friends amongst leading Italian Fascists. He and Pound tried, without success, to interest the regime in Social Credit ideas. During the War Odon Por found himself on the losing side and he disappeared into obscurity with the fall of Mussolini.[55] Ramiro de Maetzu returned to Spain and, in 1931, became editor of the Catholic and monarchist review *Acción Española*. He backed the Francoists in the Civil War, during which he was captured and shot by Republicans.[56] The fates of these two *New Age* writers, one beginning as a Syndicalist, the other as a conservative, epitomised the way in which left and right in Europe had become irretrievably polarised by the mid-1930s, so that it became difficult to remember how closely they had been intertwined in the early 1920s.

The origins of Social Credit were in the period before fascism had fully developed, and two important themes distinguished it from fascism. One was fear of centralised power. Major Douglas and his followers rejected Italian and German fascism, Soviet Communism and state intervention to modify the social effects of free markets, such as Roosevelt's New Deal and the Welfare State of post-war Britain. The second theme was opposition to the "work complex" of western civilisation. Social Crediters claimed to have a key that would unlock the storehouse of plenty for all – the problem was to free people from needless toil, not to find ways of making them work harder. Eimar O'Duffy stated this with great clarity,

> Those of us who advocate financial reform on the lines proposed by Major C. H. Douglas … believe that there is no virtue in work as such, and insist on the right of the citizen to a free choice whether he shall work or not. We reject the idea that justice requires that everybody shall do his share of the world's work and reply that the world's work will be done by those most competent to do it, who shall be highly paid in return. Finally we declare that freedom and leisure are essential to the spiritual evolution of the race and are economically possible.[57]

Most fascists recoiled from this. One example was the leading Scottish Fascist, the kilted, one-armed, former Seaforth Highlander, W.K.A.J. Chambers-Hunter, Laird of Udny and District Leader of the BUF in North East Scotland. In his *British Union and Social Credit*,[58] he praised Douglas but, like Mosley, he believed that the national dividend ought to be a reward for work, not an unearned entitlement.[59]

Social Credit in Scotland did not lead to fascism. In her anti-fascist polemic Nannie K. Wells described it as, "a great affirmative scheme, an experiment which at its very roots springs upon a denial of the fascist ideas...."[60] *The Free Man* criticised Nazi Germany for its obsession with the work complex, " we can ... emerge from a restricted and wasteful social order into a spacious and fruitful state in which economic independence would be the birthright of everyone.[61] Another Social Credit supporter, J Niven, was sceptical about Mussolini's corporations, he found it significant that, "no mention is made of the really acute problem of consumption."[62] The Glasgow Social Credit Club rejected "the doctrine of supremacy of the state" that was being promulgated in Russia, Germany and Italy. "... Men are real, the state is an abstraction behind which lurks a tyrannical power."[63]

Brainless Anti-Semitism

Although Social Credit must be distinguished from fascism, it did have a dark side. Paul Selver gave an unflattering portrait of the Major. "He was squat and bald, with a foghorn voice and somewhat Jewish appearance. This detail imparted a touch of burlesque to his brainless anti-Semitism."[64] Douglas habitually used the chopped logic and verbal circumlocutions typical of the anti-Semite. An example was the code words he used in *Warning Democracy*, "I have come to the conclusion that we are witnessing a gigantic attempt, directed from sources which have no geographical nationality, to dispossess a defective democracy and to substitute a dictatorship of Finance for it.[65] Only the naive could have misunderstood the phrase "no geographical nationality", or why the word "Finance" was given a capital letter.

In 1924, he referred to the notorious *Protocols of the Elders of Zion*. For him, the authenticity of this "scheme for the enslavement of the world" was not important.

> It is quite possible that this document is inductive rather than deductive ... that some person of great but perverted talents, with a sufficient grasp of the existing social mechanism saw and exploited the automatic results of it. If that be the case, the world owes a debt of gratitude to that mysterious author. He was substantially accurate in his generalised facts, and the inductive prophecies from them are moving rapidly towards fulfilment.[66]

In other words, either it was an authentic document or it was a forgery. If it was genuine it proved the existence of the Jewish conspiracy. But if it was invented it was an accurate reflection of what was going on beneath the surface. In either case it proved the existence of a Jewish conspiracy.

J.L. Finlay doubted that Douglas was anti-Semitic "in the normal sense"[67] because the Major believed that the problem was the exclusiveness of the Jews, which created a homogenous race that "tended to think in the same overall way." This made them "unwilling and unknowing dupes of the conspiracy not the conspiracy itself." Finlay pointed out that Douglas believed something very similar about the Freemasons so that, "to Douglas Jewishness was not a racial term at all, but a philosophical description."[68] It is difficult to see what could be a more normal form of anti-Semitism than belief in *The Protocols*, which had been exposed as a forgery in August 1921.[69] The Major must have been aware of this, hence his allowance that the document might be "deductive." But, for him, the evidence that there was no conspiracy was proof of how deeply the conspiracy had been hidden.

Some Social Credit adherents were anti-Semites and other supporters marched about in coloured shirts, but this should not lead to facile generalisations. None of the anti-Semites wore shirts and none of the shirt wearers were anti-Semitic. The Green Shirts had Jewish members and Hargrave deliberately sent one of them to Mosley's headquarters with a reply to a complaint about their anti-fascist activities.[70] Their newspaper, *Attack*, declared "JOIN THE GREEN SHIRTS AND WIPE OUT FASCISM!"[71] When Blackshirts attacked the Liverpool Green Shirts the *New Age* defended them, the "black shirt ... menaces people" with a "subtraction from their rights" but the green one was worn to "remind people of their rights" [72] Aberhart, a fundamentalist Protestant, condemned the Jews for rejecting Christ and he believed that there was a financial conspiracy, but he did not think that it was necessarily Jewish.[73] And the explanations of Douglasism by H. M. Murray and Arthur E. Powell[74] did not resort to anti-Semitism.

Sinister Influences

In 1963 MacDiarmid admitted that "the increasingly extreme anti-Semitism of Major Douglas himself ruined the movement."[75] But he did not make this criticism in the 1930s, and there is evidence that he was not free from the same prejudice. Towards the end of *Albyn* he called for a, "flanking movement against the Powers of Finance." And later in the book he wrote, "Let us not fight with enemies – England, commercial Calvinism, 'Progress,' thought-hating democracy – which are merely the agents of the foe that is really worthy of our steel, the cause that lies behind them al … "[76] If this had come from the Major, the passage could only have been read as an anti-Semitic code, but MacDiarmid did not usually write in code.

He was vulnerable to anti-Semitic prejudices. In 1911, in a letter to Ogilvie, he referred to attacks by striking miners on local Jews in Tredager, which had spread to neighbouring towns. He had attended a meeting at which the riots were organised and claimed to have discovered "an almost incredibly inhuman system of rack renting and blood-sucking on the part of the Jews in the district."[77] However, this was written by a very young man who was responding to immediate events, and he did not relate the South Wales incidents to any wider notion of a Jewish conspiracy.

In 1928 he criticised Sir Herbert Samuel, who was a candidate for Rector of Glasgow University:

> Samuel is a Jew. Asquith … comments with astonishment on Samuel's intense Jewish nationalism, his hopes for the Zionist movement. Samuel at all events, cannot fail to realise the ignominy of Scotland preferring such as himself or Baldwin, to anyone with a genuine love for, and knowledge of, his native country. What interest has Samuel in Scotland? None; but he … would not like to see his own people treated as his type treat Scotland.[78]

This was a criticism of Samuel's inconsistency as a Zionist nationalist, who rejected Scottish independence, and it was not directly an attack on his Jewishness. But in "Sentimental Nationalism" MacDiarmid wrote:

> International Finance is bent upon destroying the sub-conscious (the race memory) of all peoples and making them incapable of creative reaction against the Zeitgeist. Everything is to be sacrificed to the illusion of Progress and the sub-conscious elements capable of throwing up any effective cultural challenge to it put permanently out of commission by the destruction of all traditional communities.[79]

The point of the article was to warn about the superficiality of linguistic and cultural revivalists who took no account of the influence of international financiers. It paralleled the anti-Semitic idea that capitalist cosmopolitanism was trying to undermine authentic national identities. He did not explicitly identity the phenomenon as Jewish, but many of his readers would have mentally inserted the word.

There was an unambiguously anti-Semitic statement in *The Free Man* of September 3rd 1932. "There is no doubt" he wrote:

that in Germany there is an exceedingly powerful anti-Jewish feeling, and this is based upon the belief that the financial system of the world is run by Jews and deliberately operated to set Gentiles in opposition to each other.... so far no adequate and authoritative denial has been made by the Jews. It is true there are thousands of poor Jews, it is true that Jews have suffered much, and it is true that no man should suffer unjustly. Yet the conviction is alive in some quarters ... that sinister influences lie behind the notorious financial power of leading Jews and ... are inimical to the peace and true prosperity of the world.

He went on to quote from an article by Lord Melchett, (formerly Sir Alfred Mond), in *The Daily Herald* "A sort of mysterious and mystic power is often ascribed to the Jewish people because of their association with finance and particularly international finance ... the myth ... is rapidly fading in the light of increased knowledge". MacDiarmid responded

Does his Lordship know of any new financial system, for as yet the world knows it not? ... whatever the ruling classes of two centuries ago thought does not greatly matter, but what thousands of people in Europe still think does. They think the accusation we have mentioned has still to be met ... "[80].

Clearly he was disposed to believe in Jewish manipulation and, replying to William Aitken, he wrote:

I think, as a Douglasite, that the Jewish race has developed a particular genius in regard to finance which is a curse and a menace to humanity as a whole, and, as a Communist, I think it is not illogical to hate, and to try to exterminate such Jews just as I regard it as legitimate and necessary for proletarians ... to exterminate the intelligentsia from whom they derived that knowledge and efficiency which enables them to do, or contemplate doing, anything of the sort.[81]

He was reflecting a widespread belief about Jewish involvement in finance and he was using extreme language. But he did stress that not all Jews should be regarded as culpable. It should be noted that this was written at a time when he was approaching a psychological breakdown and he was writing in similarly extravagant language about other issues.

There was a fundamental difference between MacDiarmid's world outlook and that of Douglas. In *Economic Democracy* the Major wrote about:

> ... the agelong struggle between freedom and authority, between external compulsion and internal initiative, in which all the command of resources, information, religious dogma, educational system political opportunity and, even apparently economic necessity, is ranged on the side of authority; and ultimately authority is now exercised through finance.[82]

Douglas's underlying philosophy was highly individualistic, the problem of contemporary society could, he suggested,

> ... be summarised as a claim for the complete subjection of the individual to an objective which is externally imposed on him; which it is not necessary or even desirable that he should understand in full; and the forging of a social, industrial and political organisation which will concentrate control of policy while making effective revolt completely impossible, and leaving its originators in possession of supreme power.[83]

This fear of an external, uncontrollable, power could easily give rise to a belief in conspiracy theories. And anti-Semitism fitted closely with the Major's ideas about the financial system. The *Protocols* forgery works by exploiting the fear felt by isolated individuals who sense that others are secretly rigging the world in their own interests, Douglas dealt with this fear by becoming "Jew Wise", (to use a term of approval amongst anti-Semites). He prided himself on being able to discern the tentacles of the Jewish conspiracy that were hidden to, what he supposed to be, less astute minds.

MacDiarmid was also susceptible to conspiracy theories, but they were usually about the English establishment and its Scottish collaborators. And he applied such ideas to specific aspects of Scottish politics, they were not an over-arching explanation for all the nation's ills. And, above all, he blamed blinkered Scots for their country's subordination, not Jews. Like many in the inter-war years, he gave credence to the idea of a Jewish financial conspiracy and he can be criticised for not rising above a common prejudice. But he had never been a Syndicalist, a Guild Socialist or Functionalist. The ideas that led some of the *New Age* writers towards fascism had little relevance for him. He overlooked Douglas's anti-Semitism for too long, but he was never infected by the Major's obsession with Jewish manipulation. And, apart from the brief episode in Tredager, he never supported the persecution of Jews.

NEP Adjustments

When he became a Communist, MacDiarmid continued to support Social Credit. Marxist and Douglasite economics did have similar objectives – to explain why the few are rich while the many are poor – but they had very different analyses. Marx argued that all wealth is derived from the value created by the labour of workers, who produce commodities to be sold on the market. Inequity arises because "surplus value" has been generated within the productive process and the capitalists appropriate this, as their property, despite the fact that has been socially produced. It is then accumulated in the form of capital, which finances further production. This concentrates capital in fewer and fewer hands, continually increases the disparity in wealth in capitalist society, and subjects the working class to ever more intense exploitation.

For Douglas, inequity arose because the banks have a monopoly of credit and use this to deny consumers the full amount of the purchasing power they need, forcing them to borrow the shortfall from the banks. This creates economic depression and increases indebtedness to the bankers, who become rich while everyone else becomes poor. For Marx, in other words, exploitation was rooted in the productive process, for Douglas it was a consequence of the financial system.

And Douglas believed that money only has value in the minds of human beings, it is, " ... purely psychological, and consequently there is no limit to the amount of money except a psychological limit."[84] But Marx believed that money was the abstract expression of a real thing and it only has value when there is wealth, in the form of capital created by labour, to back it. That is why the Communist theoretician Maurice Dobb predicted, with the same certainty as any bourgeois economist, that Social Credit would produce rampant inflation.

MacDiarmid's position was less outrageous at the level of economic practice. Marx had predicted a future world in which money would be abolished. Everyone would labour according to their ability and be provided for according to their needs. But his economic theory could not be used to measure the value of particular commodities, at particular times, in any system that still relied on exchange. Lenin recognised this problem when the USSR adopted the New Economic Policy (NEP), to stimulated agriculture by reintroducing a limited market. And Soviet industry found that it had to adopt a proto-market mechanism for dealings between state enterprises. Under Stalin the system bore, "a partial resemblance to the operation of private business organisations in Western economies."[85]

MacDiarmid believed that this system was a constraint on the USSR's economic progress and that the Soviet Communists ought to abandon their theory of money.

> I agree with A. R. Orage that the Soviet system is still unfortunately working within the limits of the existing financial system and has not faced up to the fact that Douglasism has knocked the bottom out of the whole economic problem.... The warped mental processes which result in purely traditional and doctrinaire positions will ... be liquidated as soon as money is regarded ... simply as a function, and Douglasism is seen not to be an idea at variance with Communism but as a technique equally available under Capitalism or Communism just as physical functions such as breathing are.[86]

The Soviet Union ought to

> ... to get rid of its 'NEP' adjustments and other compromises with circumambient 'Capitalism,' and its terrible 'puritanical' circumscription to the theory of 'all must work' ... which tends to make it not Communism proper but simply a further logical development of Capitalism.[87]

Social Credit and Marxism had another important parallel. Marx taught that capitalism's drive to accumulate surplus value marginalized other aspects of human existence. As Shlomo Avineri puts it.

> ... Marx says ... that political economy, 'despite its wordly and pleasure seeking appearance is ... the most moral of sciences. Its principal thesis is the renunciation of life and human needs.' This asceticism is the ultimate ideological expression of alienation....[88]

"Asceticism" was a key charge Douglas made against the existing financial system and, in 1933, MacDiarmid declared that the misery of the unemployed was unnecessary:

> Whole masses of people are forced to starve or semi-starve and to stint themselves in all manner of ways in the midst of unparalleled abundance owing to this blind adherence to an obsolete system and the rooted prejudices it produces ... There is no need for economy. On the contrary an enormous increase of prosperity for everybody is immediately practicable.[89]

A Cornucopia Of Abundance

Social Credit, like Marxism, predicted a future world without drudgery. MacDiarmid expressed its humanist vision in February 1933, "we are freeing ourselves of the curse of Calvinism". Douglas's economics challenged "the whole system of 'rewards and punishments' and their insistence on the economic insanity of poverty in the midst of plenty, and drudgery within the potentiality of the Leisure State."[90] In his BBC broadcast of 1956 he said that automation of production vindicated Douglas's proposal for a national dividend:

> The automatic factories are not going to be able to buy the goods they make, nor are the people displaced by the machines.... We should then make what is physically possible financially possible too, and money would be a ticket for goods system accurately reflecting real wealth and production instead of being, as now, a commodity kept scarce for the benefit of a handful of credit monopolists and power-mongers.[91]

In his message to the *Partick East Social Credit Courier* he compared Social Credit with the fight for social justice of "Keir Hardie and the socialist pioneers":

> We are pot bound in an arbitrary and artificial financial system that has no correspondence with reality. That is why we have credit squeeze, dear money policy, unemployment and hardship, when Science has opened up perspectives abundance for all.[92]

This was another version of the utopian socialism of his ILP and Fabian youth. So when his *Albyn* strategy failed, when Social Credit did not take off as a political force and when he was excluded from the National Party of Scotland, it was logical for him to return to the left wing attitudes of his earlier years and become a Communist.

Notes

1. *Collected Poems op. cit.* Vol. I, p. 554.
2. Andrew Marr, *The Making of Modern Britain,* London, Macmillan, 2009, p. 289.
3. H. M. M., (H. M. Murray), *An Outline of Social Credit*, London, New Age Press, 1929.
4. *Ibid.*, p. 6.
5. Based on C. H. Douglas and A. R. Orage, *Credit Power and Democracy,* London, Cecil Palmer, 1920, pp. 37–47.

6. *Raucle Tongue, The II*, pp. 2289–90.
7. *An Outline of Social Credit*. p. 12.
8. David Ogg in *New Scotland,* 21 December 1935.
9. The Duke of Bedford, *The Financiers Little Game, or The Shape of Things to Come,* Glasgow, The Strickland Press, 1945, p. 3.
10. *c.f.* Elizabeth Durbin, *New Jerusalems. The Labour Party and the Economics of Democratic Socialism,* Routledge & Kegan Paul, London, Boston, Melbourne & Henley, 1985, pp. 137, 143, 182, & 220.
11. Hugh Gaitskell, "Four Monetary Heretics" in G. D. H. Cole (ed.) *What Everybody Wants to Know About Money.* Gollancz, London, 1933, p. 413.
12. Evan Durbin, *Socialism and "Social Credit",* London, The Labour Party, 1935.
13. Hugh Gaitskell, Evan Durbin and W. R. Hiskett *Socialist Credit Policy,* New Fabian Research Bureau & Victor Gollancz, 2nd ed., London, 1936, p. 11.
14. *Social Credit Discredited,* London, Martin Lawrence, 1936, pp. 12–13.
15. *The Modern Scot* July 1931.
16. GDH Cole, *Money its Present and Future*, 3rd. edn., London, Toronto, Melbourne & Sydney, Cassell, 1947, p. 340.
17. John Maynard Keynes, *General Theory of Employment Interest and Money,* Macmillan, London, 1936, *Ibid.,* p. 371.
18. CB MacPherson, *Democracy in Alberta,* University of Toronto Press, 1953, pp. 112–3.
19. *Selected Prose,* p. 116.
20. *Scottish Journal* No. 6, February, March, April 1953.
21. Lewis Grassic Gibbon & Hugh MacDiarmid (eds.) *Scottish Scene,* London, Hutchinson & Co., 1934, p. 276.
22. *Contemporary Scottish Studies*, p. 434–5.
23. *Ibid.,* p. 435.
24. *Scottish Scene,* p. 127.
25. *Letters*, p. 237.
26. *Ibid.,* p. 239.
27. *Raucle Tongue, The I*, p. 307.
28. *c.f.* Hugh MacDiarmid, *The Company I've Kept*; London, Hutchinson, 1966, pp. 105–6.
29. *Raucle Tongue, The III*, pp. 1132–4.
30. *Ibid.,* pp. 243–6.
31. *Scottish Journal* No.6, February, March, April 1953.
32. *Raucle Tongue, The III,* pp. 354–68.
33. *The Alberta Experiment*, Eyre & Spottiswood, London, 1937, pp. 83–5.
34. Andrew Marr, *The Making of Modern Britain,* p. 281.
35. See Mark Drakeford *Social Movements and their Supporters. The Green Shirts in England,* Basingstoke & New York, MacMillan, 1997 and George Thayer, *The British Political Fringe, a Profile,* London, 1965, pp. 106–113, also http://www.kibbokift.org.
36. John L. Finlay, *Social Credit the English Origins,* McGill – Queen's University Press, London & Montreal, 1972, pp. 203–4.
37. Ibid., p. 204.
38. Drakeford 1997 p. 125.
39. *c.f.* Jack Brand *The National Movement in Scotland,* Routledge & Kegan Paul London, Henley & Boston 1978, p. 204.
40. *Evening Times* 11 March 1932.
41. BLPS YMA KK/90.
42. *Scots Independent* May 1930.

43. *NLS Acc. 3721, Box 86, File 1.*

44. *Ibid.*

45. *Scots Independent,* July 1932.

46. *The Free Man* July 30th, 1932.

47. *Scots Independent.* March 1932.

48. Hugh Gaitskell, *Money and Everyday Life,* London, Labour Book Service, n.d. [circa 1939] p. 15.

49. Evan Durbin, *The Politics of Democratic Socialism,* London, George Routledge & Sons, 1940, p. 296.

50. Hugh MacDiarmid, *The Company I've Kept, op cit.,* pp. 113–4.

51. A. R. Orage (ed.), *National Guilds, an Enquiry into the Wage System and a Way Out,* London, G. Bell & Sons, pp. 63–4.

52. W. H. Greenleaf, *The British Political Tradition, Volume Two, The Ideological Heritage,* London & New York, Methuen, 1983.

53. *Authority, Liberty And Function in the Light of the War.* London, George Allen & Unwin, 1916, p. 269.

54. "Co-operation within the Corporative System of the Italian State," in *A Survey of Fascism the Year Book of the International Centre for Fascist Studies,* Vol. 1, London, Ernest Benn, 1928, p. 156.

55. See, *Ezra Pound and Italian Fascism,* pp.123, 156, 163 & 191–2.

56. http://www.britannica.com/EBchecked/topic/356325/Ramiro-de-Maeztu; Hugh Thomas, *The Spanish Civil War,* London, Eyre & Spottiswood, 1961, pp. 39–40, p. 87, p. 309.

57. Eimar O'Duffy, "The Leisure State" in *The Modern Scot,* August 1932, p. 155.

58. London, BUF, 1938.

59. See Stephen Dorril, *Blackshirt, Sir Oswald Mosley and British Fascism,* London, Viking, 2006, p. 77.

60. *The Free Man* August 26th 1933.

61. *The Free Man,* May 13, 1933.

62. *The Free Man.* February 17th 1934.

63. *Abundance* June 1937.

64. Paul Selver, *Orage and the New Age Circle.* George Allen and Unwin, London, 1959, p. 28.

65. London, C. M. Grieve, 1931, p. 62.

66. C. H. Douglas, *Social Credit,* London, C. Palmer, 1924, pp. 146–7.

67. *Social Credit the English Origins.* p. 103.

68. *Ibid.,* p. 104.

69. Norman Cohn, *Warrant for Genocide,* London, Serif, 1996, p. 171.

70. *Social Movements and their Supporters.* p. 124.

71. *Attack,* No. 32, 1935.

72. *Social Movements and their Supporters,* pp 182–3.

73. Janine Stingel, *Social Discredit. Social Credit and the Jewish Response,* Montreal, McGill-Queen's University Press, 2000, pp. 19–20.

74. Lieut. Col. Arthur E. Powell *The Deadlock of Finance,* London, Cecil Palmer, 2nd. ed. 1931.

75. *Raucle Tongue, The III,* p. 423.

76. *Albyn* p. 37.

77. *Letters,* p. 5.

78. *Raucle Tongue, The II,* pp. 69–70.

79. *Ibid.,* p. 62.

80. *Ibid.*

81. *The Free Man,* September 3rd 1932.

82. p. 79.
83. C. H. Douglas, *Economic Democracy,* London, Cecil Palmer, Third Edition, 1928, p. 10.
84. C. H. Douglas, *Warning Democracy,* London, C. M. Grieve, 1931, p. 38.
85. Harry Schwarz *The Soviet Economy Since Stalin,* London, Gollancz, 1965, p. 23.
86. *Raucle Tongue, The II,* pp. 549–50.
87. *Ibid.*
88. Shlomo Avineri, *The Social and Political Thought of Karl Marx,* Cambridge University Press, 1971, p. 110.
89. *Raucle Tongue, The II,* p. 513.
90. *Raucle Tongue, The II,* p. 344.
91. *Raucle Tongue, The III,* pp. 357–8.
92. *Partick East Social Credit Courier.* Copy kindly supplied by the University of Delaware Library.

3

Tartan

MacDiarmid and Scottish Nationalism

Lourd on my heart as winter lies
The state that Scotland's in the day
Spring in the North has aye come slow
But noo dour winter's like stay
For guid
And no for guid!

Nae wonder if I think I see
A lichter shadow than the neist
I'm fain to cry: 'The dawn, the dawn!'
I see it breakin' in the East.
But ah
Its just mair snaw!

(From *To Circumjack Cencrastus*).[1]

MacDiarmid was unlike every other Scottish nationalist, and his differences forced him out of nationalist politics on two separate occasions. Most of the other nationalists perceived Scotland as a small country, he thought it was illimitable. For them the key event in the nation's history was Bannockburn in 1314. For him Scottish history stretched back beyond recorded time. They sought inspiration in Wallace and Bruce, he rarely mentioned these heroes. They strove for popular support, he offended public opinion as a matter of principle. The intellectual range of most nationalists was limited, he continually sought for a "master idea". They imagined an independent Scotland as the country they knew, minus London government. He thought of it as a nation renewed at its roots, with its civilisation liberated from the carapace of Anglo-Scottish culture.

Scotland Shall Live!

He first became active in nationalist politics in the early 1920s, when he joined the Scottish Home Rule Association (SHRA). This was the largest self government organisation at the time and its aim was a devolved Scottish parliament achieved through legislation at Westminster. There was also a smaller organisation, the Scots National League (SNL), which wanted a complete restoration of Scottish sovereignty and secession from the UK.[2]

The National Party of Scotland (NPS) was founded in 1928, from of a merger of the SHRA, the SNL and some smaller organisations. MacDiarmid had been living in Montrose for seven years at this time and it coincided with an intensely creative period in his literary life.[3] In 1925 he published his collection of Scots lyrics *Sangschaw*, in 1926, his collection of critical essays, *Contemporary Scottish Studies*, in 1927 a second collection of Scots lyrics, *Penny Wheep* and his masterpiece, *A Drunk Man Looks at the Thistle*. Also in that year, as C. M. Grieve, he published his political polemic *Albyn*.[4]

The tone of *Albyn* was markedly less combative than that of *Contemporary Scottish Studies*, in which he had systematically attacked existing Scottish culture. It was written in response to *Caledonia*[5], by the Beaverbrook journalist George Malcolm Thomson, which had been published in the same series earlier that year. Thomson had imagined a distopian Scotland of the future, which has been taken over by Irish immigrants who have extinguished Scottish culture and driven out the native Scots. MacDiarmid fundamentally disagreed with this anti-Irish bias and he pointed out Thomson's omission of recent developments within Scottish nationalism and the need for Scotland to gain control over "credit power".[6]

However, he recommended *Caledonia* on a number of occasions,[7] as one of the few books that ascribed Scotland's parlous social and economic state to Westminster misgovernment. He also strongly agreed with Thomson in arguing that Scotland's cultural mediocrity was a mask for its economic decline. The two authors did not collide, they crossed each other's paths. The same was true of MacDiarmid and the National Party of Scotland, they met on their way to different destinations.

By the beginning of 1922, like many other members, MacDiarmid had become dissatisfied with the progress being made by the Home Rule Association and he welcomed a forceful article in the *Edinburgh Evening News* of 2nd January by Lewis Spence, Chairman of the Edinburgh Branch of the Scots National League. Spence was a journalist and the author of books on mythology and the occult, he was also a pioneer of Scots language poetry whose writings influenced MacDiarmid.

Spence's article was published less than four weeks after the Treaty that ended the Irish War of Independence, and he claimed that only fear of an extended conflict had prompted British concessions. However, a similar attitude to Scottish demands could not be assumed, "only the threat of separation will avail if we are to obtain even a minimum of self-government." He ended with a flourish:

> But enough! Let philosophers and politicians argue, but let men and patriots play the man. Let all true Scotsmen with but one spark of the tried and ancient courage of their nation stand now in her defence – or submit to race failure and be included by posterity among those peoples who were "too proud to fight" But that is unthinkable. "Scotland shall live!"

This was a bracing challenge to a country still recovering from Hogmanay and it provoked a shoal of responses, most of them opposed to Spence. But on 13th January MacDiarmid, writing as "A. K. L", expressed support.

> It is high time that gloves were taken off in this matter. How long has the Scottish Home Rule Association been in existence? – What have they done save to pass futile annual resolutions? We have a case for Scottish Home Rule indisputably, ... and it has been put fairly but ignored. I am glad to see my friend Mr. Spence coming forward ... and I hope that progress will shortly be made with the discussion of ways and means by which our demand may shortly be forced – "forced" is the word! into the forefront of practical politics.

He also criticised the SHRA for basing its appeal on "relatively trivial issues", which left the Scottish public apathetic,

> ... the real grievance is not so much in anything England has done as in what our association with such a disproportionate partner has enabled her to prevent our doing. Mere action and reaction in the sphere of existing British politics holds us to a plane upon which it is impossible to generate an effective political principle to secure anything realty worth working for. ... What is wanted – what alone will yield a real dynamic – is a separate conception of 'Scotland – a Nation' in accordance with purely Scottish psychology.[8]

The creation of the NPS gave him hope that something approximating to this vision might emerge and he gave it his full backing. As he wrote to Compton Mackenzie in April 1928,

> The country is waking up: and a new sense of nationalism is becoming very wide-spread and manifesting itself in all manner of promising ways. To gather them up and direct them to a goal is the task now: and I believe that the National Party now in process of formation will succeed in doing that.[9]

In June 1928 MacDiarmid spoke at the Party's first Bannockburn Rally, deputising for Compton Mackenzie, who had been held up by bad weather. Mackenzie had intended to call for a Celtic cultural revival,[10] but MacDiarmid took a different tack. He hailed the progress being made by the NPS and predicted that Scottish nationalism would be a live issue at the next general election. He explained that he and Mackenzie had turned down offers to stand as ILP candidates because, "For those of us forming the National Party who have hitherto been Conservatives, Liberals or Socialists, these English party divisions have lost all significance".[11] His speech was constructive because he wanted to consolidate the fledgling party, not to tear it apart. He took the same attitude at the first annual conference. He criticised the proposed Party programme for "… borrowing too much from existing conditions in English Parties", nevertheless, if it was passed, "all should be prepared to support it."[12]

Wild Men

MacDiarmid has been perceived as a consistently extreme and disruptive figure within the NPS. One reason for this was John MacCormick's *The Flag in the Wind*,[13] written many years later, which described MacDiarmid as, "one of the greatest handicaps with which any national movement could have been burdened".[14] He claimed that the poet had been one of the "wild men" who had deterred the Duke of Montrose from joining the Party.[15] MacCormick may have forgotten that, in fact, *he* had been mainly responsible for causing Montrose to break his links with the NPS.

The background to this episode was a National Covenant launched by the Party in 1930. It had declared, "We bind ourselves to act on the belief that the mandate of a majority of Scottish citizens is sufficient authority for the setting up of an independent Parliament in Scotland."[16] At the 1931 conference, MacCormick moved a resolution demanding that the British government organise a plebiscite on Home Rule. An addendum instructed the Party's National Council, in the event of a refusal by Westminster, to organise the Covenant signatories into "sections capable of running the public services of this country".[17] MacDiarmid seconded the resolution, in a more measured speech which predicted, "a tremendous amount of counter propaganda".[18] It was this decision that prompted the Duke to renounce his support for the NPS.[19]

Despite Montrose's defection, the Party achieved a good deal of momentum. In October 1931 Compton Mackenzie was elected Lord Rector by the students of Glasgow University, becoming the first ever Scottish nationalist to win an election. There were also a couple of promising by-elections results and favourable treatment from sections of the press. However this provoked a challenge from established Unionist opinion and it also prompted the formation of the Scottish Party, which stood for a devolved parliament within the UK, with Scotland sharing control of the Empire. This grouping was small in size but it included influential figures, such as the Duke of Montrose and a clutch of professors and businessmen.

The NPS at first treated these "moderates" with disdain, but it suffered a disastrous result in the East Fife by-election of January 1933, when the novelist Eric Linklater came bottom of the poll with 3.6%. This forced a retreat and confidential negotiations were opened up with the Scottish Party. John McCormick believed that only unity of the two organisations could boost the credibility of nationalist politics and his strategy seemed to be validated when they agreed to back a joint candidate in the Kilmarnock by-election of November 1933, when Sir Alexander MacEwan of the Scottish Party achieved 16.9%.

Independent National Status

The National Council submitted a revised statement of aims to the May 1933 conference, in an attempt to build a bridge to the Scottish Party. The key paragraph stated that,

> Scotland should jointly set up with England machinery to deal with those responsibilities and, in particular, with such matters as Defence and Foreign Policy and the creation of a Customs Union."[20]

A minority of the NPS rejected this. They believed that Scotland had to retrieve its sovereignty unconditionally, only afterwards would it be legitimate to decide its relations with England. Their counter-proposal was that Scotland should become a, self-governing Dominion, sovereign and equal with England.

> ... for Scotland as for all other self-governing nations of the British Commonwealth these arrangements will supersede the authority of the present Parliament at Westminster, will be subject to the respective peoples and the Parliaments concerned, and will likewise conform with Article 20 of the League of Nations, of which they are signatories.[21]

Dominion status, in other words, was a way of extricating Scotland from the sovereignty of Westminster. As the veteran nationalist Angus Clark, President of the London Branch of the NPS, put it,

> Independent national status means the freedom of the Scots people to consider and decide every question that concerns their moral, spiritual and material welfare entirely from a Scottish standpoint.... And made not by an Imperial Parliament, in a alien capital, nor by joint arrangements with England, but inside our own borders by ourselves alone.... In other words the two hundred years of England's political domination in Scotland must be finally and completely ended.[22]

This was an ideological struggle about the meaning of sovereignty, not a debate between imperialists and anti-imperialists. In fact all members of the NPS, including MacDiarmid, complained that Scotland was being denied its rightful place in the running of Imperial affairs.

The conference passed the National Council's resolution by 71 votes to 44, but the proceedings fell apart when a resolution to restate the Party's former aims was also passed, and a proposal to open negotiations with the Scottish Party was rejected. The leadership interpreted the disorder as deliberate disruption and, at the National Conference the following November, two leading oppositionists, Angus Clark and W. Dugald MacColl, were expelled and the South East Area Council was dissolved. The London Branch was suspended and it subsequently severed its connections with the Party. The opponents of a merger had been removed and, in April 1934, the two organisations united as the Scottish National Party.

An Impossible Person

Although MacDiarmid supported the proposal for Dominion status, and rejected the leadership's courting of the Scottish Party, he did not share the opposition's preoccupation with the legal status of Scottish sovereignty. What he objected to was the NPS becoming just another, compromising, political party. It shared, he claimed, the mentality it ought to destroy. "Tone and procedure" at a recent public meeting in Edinburgh were, "identical with those which prevail at the meetings of any of the English-controlled parties...." There had been, "... scarcely anything said which indicated a sense of the real issues or seemed to promise that the New Scotland stood for anything spiritually distinctive and had something substantive and vital to contribute...." Was Scotland, he asked, "to make a lesser contribution to the world, to stand for a smaller idea, than Fascism in Italy or Bolshevism in Russia?"[23] This was a significant remark, he had always believed that the proper comparators for Scotland were European, not English. But both sides in the NPS were carrying on their debate as if only Scotland, England and the Empire were relevant.

In the middle of 1929 MacDiarmid moved to London to take up the editorship of Compton Mackenzie's short-lived magazine of radio criticism, *Vox*. In July he suffered a potentially serious accident and by the following January his marriage was breaking down, it ended in a bitter divorce a year later. In May 1930 he moved to a public relations job in Liverpool, returning to Edinburgh in August 1932 with his new wife Valda and their infant son Michael. Shortly thereafter they departed for Shetland. This meant that, during its internal crisis, he could only intervene in the affairs of the NPS through his journalism, which became increasingly vituperative about the Party leadership.

He must have allowed his membership to lapse because, after his return to the capital in 1933, he wrote to MacCormick claiming that he was now a member of the South Edinburgh Branch.[24] But Party headquarters refused to register his renewal unless he gave a commitment to adhere to the Party's objects and policy. He refused, pointing out that he was not a member of any other party and that, in rejoining, he had given the normal undertakings required by NPS rules. He demanded the right to make a personal statement to the National Conference in May 1933, but this was refused. At the Conference his friend Archie Lamont moved his reinstatement but was defeated by 55 votes to 38.[25]

The delegates may have been influenced by his scathing articles and the bitter hostility with which he was regarded by some leading members, MacCormick believed that refusing MacDiarmid's readmission would, "win us hundreds of new members".[26] There were objections to his alleged membership of the Communist Party, although he was not a member at the relevant time. And, despite his public renunciation of his ILP candidature in 1928, Tom Gibson believed that he still wanted to collaborate with the Labour Party.[27] John MacCormick disliked his support for Social Credit, which he thought was, "an indirect way of mixing us up with English politics."[28] And MacDiarmid was an obstacle to the merger with the Scottish Party, George Malcolm Thomson, an influential background figure in the negotiations, consider his Douglasism to be "dangerous",[29] he also disliked MacDiarmid's pro-Irish stance, "... the non-Catholic can do things the paid agent of the Roman Catholic Church ... could not do."[30] (This was marked "confidential" – a difference between MacDiarmid and some of his opponents was that he was openly vituperative – they dripped poison in secret).

Goodbye To All That

He was now outside the National Party and he responded by staking out new ground:

> I cannot be bought or influenced in one way or another, and I will implacably pursue, in season and out of season, objectives to which the complete severance of a Soviet-Republican Scotland from England is only the merest preliminary, but if I can't do it in the sphere of practical affairs I will at least do it in some of the best poetry Scotland had produced.[31]

This refers to *Clann Albainn*, which was the name of a covert nationalist group (discussed below) and also, as Alan Riach notes, the title of a long poem to be published in a series of five books, but never completed.[32] It was the starting point of his search for a new "master idea" and it led him to Marxism.

The first volume of *Clann Albainn* was to be about "The Muckle Toon" – his birthplace Langholm – and this imaginative return enabled him see the politics of his youth in a new perspective.

> The Hymns to Lenin which have occasioned controversy have their natural part in the first book because they are in logical sequence from the radicalism of that Border burgh and my father's pronounced Trade Unionist and Co-operative sympathies, while in a wider sense the return to thoughts of Langholm and my boyhood represents a "return to the people" which has its bearing on the motives which impelled me to use Braid Scots and have led me at this stage of my career to my present political position....[33]

In his 1928 Bannockburn speech he had stressed the cross-party nature of the national movement, an independent nation, he had written in 1926, "will still accommodate Tory, Liberal and Socialist"[34] but from now on, he was firmly committed to a left wing interpretation of Scottish nationalism. The failure of his attempts to promote this within the Communist Party of Great Britain will be discussed in the next chapter, but it is appropriate, at this point, to clarify four specific issues about his nationalism. First, the nature of the organisation called "Clann Albainn", second his relationship to the Celtic nationalist ideas of Ruairidh Erskine of Mar, third his language politics and fourth his alleged Anglophobia;.

A Society To Be Known As Clann Albainn[35]

According to Compton Mackenzie, Clann Albainn was created in order to, "... raise the consciousness of the Scots by undertaking politically sensitive and illegal acts."[36]

> Ruaridh Erskine of Mar and Christopher Grieve were both in sympathy with my fear of parochialism and we discussed the possibility of forming a society to be known as Clann Albainn, the members of which would be pledged to do all they could to foster the Celtic Idea with a vision ... of rescuing the British Isles from being dominated by London.[37]

Iain Gillies must have been referring to this organisation in a letter to members of the former London Branch of the NPS of December 1933:

> A new organisation ... provides the opportunity of active service to every Nationalist of whatever talents, qualifications and experience.... Each member has to play his or her part according to ability, fulfilling a definite function in the co-ordinated plans of the movement which will challenge the Anglicisation and the subjection of Scotland, not by party-political mock tactics but by Action on constructive principles all along the line.[38]

In his "Scotland in 1980" of 1929, MacDiarmid described an imaginary Clann Albainn, which was a "militaristic neo-fascist auxiliary"[39], this may be the source for Tim Luckhurst's claim that, "McDairmid even established a Scottish fascist combat organisation, which he called Clann Albain".[40] The essay was, of course, a piece of imaginative fiction. In any case, fascist movements of the inter-war years were not secret societies they were, or aspired to be, highly visible mass movements. "Neo-fascist" nowadays refers to fascist revivalist organisations after

1945, its use in 1929 could only mean that the Clann was not a copy of German or Italian fascism. And it could not have been "militarist" because an armed movement of the 1930s would not have been open to women members, as Iain Gillies implied.

MacDiarmid claimed that Clann Albainn represented a "left wing" of the National Party and was now "forging ahead."

> ... they are making towards a wholesale Scottish Sinn Fein policy, on a dual basis of a new Gaelic and Scots vernacular culture; that they are becoming increasingly anti-English, that they will not keep within the limits of conventional methods, and that on wider issues in politics today they are vitally concerned with the English ascendancy in the British Isles and with the question of Europe versus the Empire.[41]

This was an elaboration of the proposals he had discussed with Mackenzie and Erskine and shows that Clann Albainn was a semi-secret group, with broadly Celtic revivalist aims, which was set up to engage in non-violent direct action,[42] but it never rallied any significant number of nationalists to its ranks. It was one of a number of fringe groups which MacDiarmid backed at various times, because he did not believe that a political party with a strategy of fighting elections could achieve any form of self-government worth the name. His statements about Clann Albainn were examples of his habit of presenting his own hopes and ambitions as established facts.

Celtic Ideology

MacDiarmid had a close friendship with the Catholic Highlander the Hon. Ruairidh Erskine of Mar, but the two differed on key issues. Erskine has been misunderstood as a left-wing nationalist, he did write, in 1918, "Praise to the Bolsheviks! Honour to the Revolutionaries!",[43] but what he applauded was the publication by Lenin's government of the secret war plans of Imperial Russia and its allies, and the Soviet Republic's repudiation of territorial gains through war. Erskine was too much of a Catholic to endorse the Bolshevik ideology of class struggle and international proletarian revolution.

The titles of his series on "Celtic Communism", in John MacLean's newspaper *The Vanguard*,[44] can also give a false impression. As a follower of Papal social teaching, he thought that the main virtue of ancient Celtic civilisation had been its social harmony, which had overcome class divisions, not class struggle. By "communism" he meant the decentralised, direct democracy, supposedly practiced by the pre-feudal clans. The articles were based on his reading of ancient Celtic history and, for him, the key feature of the Gaelic polity had been its plural system of government, in which,

> ... there could be no power or authority that was not balanced by some other power or authority erected for the purpose of holding power and authority in check and preventing the abuses to which unbalanced Power is apt to give rise.[45]

But the balance had been upset when the "Ard-righ" (the High King), became an hereditary ruler and created the preconditions for feudalism. This was a Scottish version of the "myth of the Norman Yoke", with Scotland's David the First standing in for England's William the Conqueror, and with Celtic clansmen instead of Anglo-Saxon freemen.

Reviewing MacDiarmid's *Albyn,* Erskine criticised him for failing to set out the, "successive steps in Scotland's fall". These "steps" had been the introduction of feudalism by David, the reinstatement of the feudal monarchy after the Wars of Independence, the Reformation and the Unions of 1603 and 1707. He also criticised *Albyn* for omitting the "broader aspects of the Celtic Movement" in Brittany, Wales and Ireland, and for not offering an analysis of "Celtic ideology."[46] This referred to his project of restoring the ancient Celtic forms of government and Erskine developed these ideas further in his *Changing Scotland* of 1931, a work which was similar to Ferris's *The Gaelic Commonwealth.*[47] Both envisioned a free nation, in which Gaelic would be restored as the national language with decentralised political institutions, under a limited monarchy. And both were similar to the conservative anti-capitalism of Hillaire Belloc's *The Servile State.*

Erskine had a long association with Irish nationalism, going back to the days of Parnell and his version of the Celtic past had similarities not only with Ferris, but with Irish Catholic writers, "... like Darrell Figgis, Aodh de Blácam, Father Patrick Coffey", who all, "fantasised about a 'Gaelic State', seen as a decentralised, egalitarian, frugally moral federation of artisans and smallholders".[48]

Erskine Ferris and Figgis[49] saw the Gaelic state as a matter of organisation – of recreating a polity based on a network of small communities, with limits on the sovereignty of the higher organs of government. And both Erskine and Ferris saw the restoration of Gaelic civilisation as a conscious turning back to the political forms of the past, but MacDiarmid thought of Gaelic civilisation as point of departure for thinking about the politics of the contemporary world.

The Common People of Scotland

This difference can be seen in their attitudes to Jacobitism. Erskine believed that the outcome of the Battle of Culloden had been a defeat for the Scottish nation, which could only be reversed by breaking with the reigning dynasty and establishing an independent, constitutional, monarchy within a Gaelic state. MacDiarmid's only substantial writing on the subject was "A Scots Communist Looks at Bonnie Prince Charlie"[50] published on the bi-centenary of the '45 Rebellion. His chief target was the anti-nationalism of the Scottish Communists, but it is possible to extract from it evidence about his attitude towards Jacobitism.

Scotland's literature in Gaelic, Scots and English, he argued, all showed the same "technical devices and aesthetic effects". And the "great pronouncements" of Roman Catholics, Protestant Reformers and Covenanters had disclosed the "same identity". Their differences had been exaggerated because English government had prevented them from joining issue on great Scottish questions, and this had confined them to smaller matters. But the so-called "dream and fakery" of the '45 had, "produced a great outpouring of poetry by men like Alasdair MacMhaighstir Alasdair and Iain Rhuach Stiubhairt....

> And today the same essential cause is producing a like result; another efflorescence of the Scottish genius in Gaelic and our other tongues. *There can be no minimising the high significance of a cause, (however, romantic and unreal it may seem to be to those "practical people" who have brought us to so sorry a pass) which contains such inexhaustible revolutionary momentum as to reappear with renewed vitality after being suppressed for a couple of centuries of unparalleled change.*[51]

MacDiarmid detested those Communists who labelled as "progressive" the bourgeois state that had efficiently crushed the clans. He believed that retrieving the culture the '45 would be part of a rediscovery of Scotland's lost identity and, in this, he was influenced by the same ideas about the Celtic past as Erskine and Ferris. He agreed, in particular, with Erskine's claim that the original rights of the Scottish people, within the clan system, had been usurped when their kings imported English feudalism. But his conclusions were modern, the recently re-established Highland Land League must seek,

> ... the backing of the common people of Scotland – not the businessmen and professional men who are the mainstay of the

present system.… All that sort of thing must be swept away, and we must get back to those real roots which were the source of our national strength in the past and remain our only hope for the future.[52]

Erskine believed that Scotland ought to revert to the political apparatus of its Celtic past, but MacDiarmid believed that the essence of the Celtic political system could only be revived in a modern socialist and republican form and with twentieth century economic theory, not through a reversion to a semi-mythical Celtic arcadia.

The Task of Reviving a Language

Erskine believed that Scotland must revert to being a Gaelic speaking country. He excoriated those, like Yeats, who argued that Gaelic "beauties of word and phrase, of idea and myth and legend" could survive when expressed through English. Such people were "mentally lazy" and would not be "at the pains to learn Gaelic".[53] But the difficulties of reviving Gaelic as a vernacular were shown by the Irish Free State's attempts to do so. In 1927 a scholar warned that,

> The task of reviving a language … with no large neighbouring population which speaks even a distantly related dialect, and with one of the great world-languages to contend with, is one that has never been accomplished anywhere. Analogies with Flemish, Czech, or the Baltic languages are all misleading, because the problem in their cases has rather been that of restoring a peasant language to cultivated use than that of reviving one which the majority has ceased to speak.[54]

In 1949 Ernest Blythe, Director of Dublin's Abbey Theatre, reflected on the progress of the Irish language movement. More than forty years earlier he had been a pioneer of the Gaelic League, but he looked back with ruthless honesty.

> Very soon after the Black and Tan period, a prominent public man said that not more than a dozen individuals, out of the scores of thousands who had joined [Gaelic League] Branch classes, had learned enough Irish to speak it with reasonable fluency and accuracy. Of course, in mentioning a dozen he gave too low a figure If he had said two hundred, however, I do not think he would have been far wrong.[55]

The Gaelic League's efforts had created good will for the language, but most of those who enlisted in its classes dropped out when they discovered how difficult it was to become reasonably proficient. Another, purely practical, difficulty had been the lack of interest which native speakers took in preserving the language and the character of the literature and text books in Irish, which reflected the life of the rural Ireland of the West, not Irish urban society.[56]

When MacDiarmid visited Dublin in 1928, invited to attend the Tailtean Games by Oliver St John Gogarty, he saw little evidence of an Irish language revival. "There was a considerable measure of enthusiasm for the revival of Gaelic prior to the Treaty, but the Gaelic encouraging policy of the Government has practically killed it off. It could only thrive in an atmosphere of opposition." W. B. Yeats and Gogarty told him that the new state was, "at present in the trough of the wave",

> The impetus that led to its establishment and the Irish Literary revival has spent itself.... The abnormal efflorescence of Irish genius could not be maintained: the immediate future must be relatively mediocre. What are needed now are not poets and fiery propagandists and rebel leaders, but administrators, economists and practical experts.[57]

Unlike the Gaelic revivalists, he was not interested in replacing one language with another, he was interested in extending the range and complexity of language itself, as a cultural and psychological medium. This was, as Roderick Watson puts it, "a vision of the world *of* language and also the world *as* language."[58] And he also believed that the revival of Gaelic required a new political context.

> Even Gaelic enthusiasts are ... willing only to 'think' about a Gaelic movement while remaining for the most part within the circle of the very conditions responsible for the progressive desuetude of the Gaelic language and all that once connoted. They are so pathetically anxious to impress people as being 'reasonable'.... Words like 'Communism', 'Revolution' etc., have become hopeless bogies to them. But it is utter folly to talk about reviving the Gaelic without appreciating that the Gaelic cannot be restored except by restoring social and economic conditions appropriate to it. It cannot be re-introduced and adapted to the existing system the whole tendency of which has been responsible for its steady attenuation.[59]

That was why he criticised the proposal of the Vernacular Circle of the London Burns Club to revive Lowland Scots. In 1921 it commissioned a series of lectures on the Scots language by prominent exiles and a collection of four of these were published.[60] MacDiarmid attacked J.M. Bulloch's essay, "The Delight of the Doric in the Diminutive." This suggested that the psychology of the Scots was reflected in the use of the diminutive forms of words, a characteristic of the North East dialect. For MacDiarmid this was "infantilism", the Vernacular Circle,

> … emphasises the part at the expense of the whole, and puts the cart before the horse. Had the aim been to encourage all that is finest and best in Scottish literature, whether written in Doric or English, the movement might have merited some support – although after all prizes do not produce literature.[61]

And he endorsed the idea, rejected by Erskine, that the essence of the "Scottish mentality" could be expressed through English.

> Synge, Yeats, and other great Irish writers found no difficulty in expressing themselves in English which they yet made distinctively Irish. Is the psychological difference between, say, Oscar Wilde and Joseph Conrad not as profound as the difference between an Englishman and a Scot?[62]

However, the Vernacular Circle's volume also contained an essay by W. A. Craigie, who was Professor of Anglo-Saxon in the University of Oxford and a founder of the Oxford English Dictionary. Craigie asked:

> Can you imagine a complete grammar of Lowland Scots, written throughout in that language? The Frisians and Faeroese have done that for their tongues. Can you imagine a work on Botany written throughout in the Scottish tongue? There is one in Faeroese. If anyone doubts the possibility of recreating a literary tongue, capable of expressing all the necessary ideas which must occur in dealing with literature, history, science, and even philosophy, I will direct him to what has been written in the new Norwegian tongue within the past twenty years.

He suggested that Scots could be revived on the model of New Norwegian, Frisian and Faeroese. In each of these cases a language of low status had been redeveloped as a literary medium. None had a standard spelling and there was no written form of Faeroese. But they had been resurrected. with a standard grammar and orthography, and had been used for a wide range of literature.[63]

MacDiarmid agreed with Craigie that the revival of the Scots language could be part of a modern Scottish nationhood, but he did not advocate the Scandinavian model, which required the expert work of linguists. He preferred to start with the resources that already existed, in the fragmented remains of Lowland Scots. This was because he believed that the recapture of one part of Scotland's national existence must lead to the recovery of all of it.

Alan Bold, has described how he was forced to rethink his view of a Scots language revival when Lewis Spence published an experimental poem, of high literary quality.[64] This prompted him to experiment with writing in Scots, using a vocabulary drawn from Sir James Wilson's *Lowland Scotch as Spoken in the Lower Strathearn District of Perthshire*.[65] (The book had an introduction by Craigie). He later described what had happened as a, "satori ... an illumination, a sudden awakening"[66] He now believed that a literature in Scots would lead to the kind of national revival advocated by the Gaelic revivalists, but this would be achieved by a cultural Renaissance, not through state action from above. And since he believed that there was a natural affinity between literature in Scots, in Gaelic, and in the Norn of Orcadian and Shetland writers, his programme implied linguistic plurality.

A political project of re-establishing Gaelic as the vernacular of Scotland would only have been possible if the Gaels, a geographical and cultural minority, had succeeded in imposing their will on the majority. MacDiarmid's language politics helped to get Scottish nationalists off the hook of Erskine's Gaelic fundamentalism. In this measure, he contributed to the political moderation of the movement, (which is not to imply that he intended such an outcome.)

Ill-behaved English Sailors

In *Who's Who* MacDiarmid listed his hobby as "Anglophobia"[67]. This was jocular[68] (he had no hobbies to list), but it has helped to give credence to the idea that he was prejudiced against the English nation. John MacCormick castigated his, "extravagant and self-assertive criticism of the English"[69] but he did not quote anything MacDiarmid actually said, and no complaints about his attitudes have been recorded by aggrieved English people.[70]

The 1922 exchange in the *Edinburgh Evening News* offers a useful perspective. Lewis Spence was a thoroughgoing Anglophobe. As a "student of racial science",[71] he believed that the English were mainly of Iberian, Belgian, Saxon and Danish origins, while most Scots were of Pictish ancestry,[72] this made the English as different from the Scots as the French from the Germans.[73] The 1921 census had shown a significant increase in the numbers of English born residents in Scotland and Spence forecast that, if this "English invasion" continued for another fifty years, "Scotsmen will have become so impregnated with English ideas and so mingled with English blood as to have lost all semblance of a separate nationality."[74]

The English had infiltrated the universities, civil service and local government and "ill-behaved English sailors" and "English artistes" were a threat to Scottish morals. The Highlands were being overrun by, "a debased cosmopolitan plutocracy" and the "best blood" was being driven from the soil so that "London Jews and English 'backwoodsmen' may play at shooting tame deer!" Home Rule was no solution because the English elite would "not allow their playground to slip from their grasp."[75]

MacDiarmid subtly distanced himself from this blood and soil rhetoric. Anglophobia, he wrote, was "no essential element of the Scottish Free State Movement", although it was "still very widespread in Scottish hearts" and, during the war, "all sorts of racial antipathies" had flared up from time to time amongst the Allied forces.[76] In other words the antipathy was not universal, it arose only in particular circumstances. And he quoted from *England and the New Era*, by Brougham Villiers.

> It would be a misfortune if the vigorous nationality of Scotland ... were merged in that of England; as an Englishman, I should naturally think it worse of the opposite result came about and we all became Scotsmen. Neither is at all likely, though I fear there can be no question that English national feeling has decayed or been merged in the Imperialist fever far more than that of Scotland.[77]

"Brougham Villiers" was the Tyneside journalist Frederick John Shaw, a Fabian and a campaigner for women's suffrage. He predicted an upsurge in national consciousness amongst the nations of the UK and the Empire, following the War. This would mean a new and progressive sense of English nationality and he stressed that the "England" of his title did not mean "the United Kingdom as a whole".[78] He did not believe that Scotland and Wales would want to separate, but the three nations should be allowed to develop in their own ways, "on terms not 'planned' by Whitehall but worked out by free agreement between the peoples.... "[79] Lewis Spence could never have accepted the notion of a progressive England, but MacDiarmid, like Villiers, believed that antagonism between the two nations was cultural, not racial.

Frontier Spirit

Willa Muir remembered that, as a Borderer, he "blamed the 'Eng-glish' for the whole of Scotland's backwardness in the arts."[80] He confirmed this in 1968 when he remembered that he had shared fully in Langholm's "frontier spirit" and its "general dislike of everything English," which was also a "determined resistance to assimilation to English standards." This meant the "virtual monopoly" of English literature in his education, and punishment of schoolchildren for lapsing into Scottish idioms.[81] That was why, when he returned from the First World War,

> ... I applied myself to understand the position and acquire a definite idea of Scotland was.... After all we were fighting for the rights of small nations ... and when I came back I discovered to my horror that I didn't know anything about Scotland and had never been taught anything about Scots literature.[82]

This suggests that in his youth he had absorbed an immature prejudice against the English and, in later years, he liked to strike poses, amongst which were exaggerated attacks on the English. But in his creative work he was mainly concerned with understanding, analysing and criticising Scotland, not with anathematising England.

In *Aesthetics in Scotland* he expressed a grievance about the English cultural establishment and its belated recognition of Scottish painting.

> It did not occur to any of them, however, to examine more deeply this extraordinary situation in which two countries linked together under a common Crown and Parliament for two and a half centuries one of them remained utterly ignorant of, and indifferent to, so important a part of the other's life as its paintings.[83]

This was written as part of a polemic in which he also excoriated the Scots, the "vast majority" of whom were, "as ignorant as the English with regard to the Scottish tradition in literature and the arts, and, indeed with regard to Scottish interests in the whole range of affairs."[84] He wanted to alert Scots to the dilution of their culture by the numerical domination of England within the Union. To this end he often exaggerated or caricatured English attitudes and intentions. But his primary target was the Anglified Scots, not the English nation.

An article of 1948 provides some clarification of his later attitudes:

> ... the overwhelming consensus of opinion against the English on the score of their greed, their stupidity, their cruelty, their snobbery, and all the rest of it cannot be lightly set aside as due simply to envy or counter-propaganda. It is, in fact, a detestation of the English which is thoroughly well founded and which arises basically from the fact that the English, like their cousins the Germans, have a *'herren volk'* tradition and are intolerably arrogant and overbearing.[85]

This was a cruder version of the Apollonian/Faustian dichotomy he had put forward in *Albyn,* as is made clear in a later passage.

> I do not like the English. I do not admire the part they played in history or the part they are playing in it today. I believe that we ought to foster all those elements in our natures and traditions which are at the furthest remove from anything English. Furthermore I believe the English are finished as a world power and must be forced back on their 'right little tight little island' – or rather that part of it that is their own.[86]

In 1927 he believed that the Spenglerian cycle was going to consign England to rapid decline, while raising up Scotland. By 1949 this prediction had not been fulfilled, and his rhetoric had coarsened. But the article quoted above was a critique of James Bridie and Moray Maclaren, both of whom had expressed a liking for their southern neighbours. In other words, it was mainly directed against fellow Scots, not against the English. He believed there was a fundamental cultural cleavage between the two nations, and he wanted to rally resistance to the pressures he believed were crushing Scotland's identity. But he placed responsibility for this on those Scots who accepted their nation's subordinate status. His primary struggle was not against England, it was against the mainstream of Scottish culture and politics.

Notes

1. *Collected Poems pp.* 204–5.
2. For histories of Scottish Nationalism see Brand, 1978, Finlay c1994, Hanham 1969, Harvie 1974 & MacCormick 1955.
3. For a discussion of the cultural significance of Montrose at this time see Robert Crawford, "MacDiarmid in Montrose", Alex Davis & Lee M. Jenkins, *Locations of Literary Modernism, Region and Nation in British and American Modernist Poetry,* Cambridge University Press, 2000, pp. 33–56.

4. *Albyn; or, Scotland and the Future,* Kegan Paul, Trench, Trübner and Co. London and New York, 1925.
5. *Caledonia or the Future of the Scots,* Kegan Paul, Trench, Trübner and Co. London and New York, 1927.
6. *Raucle Tongue, The II,* pp. 26–7.
7. *Raucle Tongue, The II,* pp. 26–7, 69, 163, 202, 257.
8. *Contemporary Scottish Studies* p. 304.
9. *Letters* p. 388.
10. His telegram to the rally, giving the gist of the speech he had intended to make, is in the Muirhead Papers NLS Acc. 3721, Box 8, File 160.
11. Reproduced in Gordon Wright, *Hugh MacDiarmid an Illustrated Biography,* Gordon Wright Publishing, Edinburgh, 1977, pp. 48.
12. NLS Dep. 209, Box 15, Folder 1.
13. John MacCormick, *The Flag in the Wind, The Story of the National Movement in Scotland,* London, Victor Gollancz, 1955.
14. *Ibid.,* p. 35.
15. *Flag in the Wind,* p. 35.
16. Quoted in Arthur Turner, *Scottish Home Rule,* Blackwell, Oxford, 1952, p. 10 & H. J. Hanham, *Scottish Nationalism,* London, Faber and Faber, 1969, p. 158.
17. *Scots Independent* June 1931.
18. *Ibid.*
19. Letter to the *Glasgow Herald* 13th May 1931.
20. Quoted in Brand (1978), p. 222 & Finlay (1994), p. 153.
21. NLS Acc. 3721, Box 86, File 1.
22. *The Free Man,* 11 November 1933.
23. *The Free Man* 8 October 1932.
24. *New Selected Letters,* p. 51.
25. NLS Acc. 3721 Box 86, File 1.
26. NLS Acc. 6058, Box 1, File 4.
27. Letter to Neil Gunn, 11 April 1933, letter to George Dott 30 April 1933, NLS Acc. 6058 Box 1, File 4.
28. *Ibid.*
29. Undated letter to George Dott [probably July or August 1930] NLS Acc. 5927, Box I, Folder 1.
30. Letter to George Dott August 1930, *Ibid.,* Folder 3.
31. *The Free Man* July 1932.
32. Alan Riach (ed.), *Hugh MacDiarmid's Epic Poetry,* Edinburgh University Press, 1991, pp. 9–14.
33. *The Scots Observer,* 12 August 1933.
34. *Contemporary Scottish Studies* p. 304.
35. This title was spelled in a number of ways by MacDiarmid and others at the time, for clarity I have standardised it.
36. Andro Linklater, *Compton Mackenzie a Life,* London, Hogarth Press, 1992, p. 234.
37. Compton Mackenzie, *My Life and Times, Octave Six, 1923–1930,* London, Chatto & Windus, 1967, p. 189.
38. NLS Acc. 6058, Box 1, File 4.
39. *Albyn* p. 77.
40. *The Independent* 6 March 2002.
41. *Daily Record* 10th May 1930.
42. A "Clann Albainn Society" was proposed in 1948, with the aim of acquiring and settling a "deserted glen" in the West Highlands, to grow foodstuffs in short supply – nothing seems to have come of this initiative *(Scots Independent April 1948).*

L. to R. Hugh MacDiarmid, Oliver Brown and Dr Ian Taylor at a press conference in the Doric Hotel, Minto Street, Edinburgh, to launch the 1320 Club and the Club's magazine 'Catalyst'. December 1967. (Gordon Wright)

Major F A C Boothby, editor and publisher of 'Sgian Dubh: The News-letter of the National Movement' with Hugh MacDiarmid, photo-graphed outside MacDiarmid's home, Brownsbank, in March 1975. (Gordon Wright)

Hugh MacDiarmid addresses a 1320 Club symposium at Glasgow University, 6 April 1968. (Gordon Wright)

Christopher Murray Grieve (nom de plume, 'Hugh MacDiarmid'), from
the series 'The Seven Poets' by Jessie Ann Matthew – Scottish National
Portrait Gallery.

Christopher Murray Grieve (nom de plume, 'Hugh MacDiarmid') by
Alexander (Sandy) Moffat – Scottish National Portrait Gallery

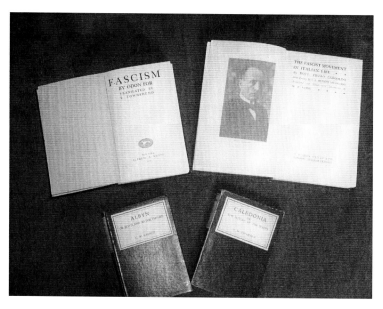

Four key books from the 1920s. (Author)

43. *Guth na Bliadhna,* An t-Earrach [Spring] 1918, p. 97.
44. September- December 1920.
45. *The Vanguard* December 1920.
46. *The Pictish Review*, Vol. 1, No. 2, December 1927.
47. Montrose, The Review Press. This book has some similarities to Ferris's *The Gaelic Commonwealth,* but it is probable that this arises from their use of the same sources.
48. Patrick Maume, *The Long Gestation: Irish Nationalist Life, 1891–1918*, Dublin, Gill & Macmillan, 1999, p. 208.
49. See his *The Gaelic State in the Past and the Future, or "The Crown of a Nation",* Dublin, Maunsel & Co, 1917.
50. *Scots Independent* August 1945.
51. *Ibid.,* italics in original.
52. *Ibid.*, p. 186.
53. In Margery Palmer McCulloch, (ed.) *Modernism and Nationalism: Literature and Society in Scotland 1918–1939, Source Documents for the Scottish Renaissance,* Glasgow, The Association for Scottish Literary Studies, 2004, pp. 294–5.
54. Professor Michael Tierney, quoted in Terence Brown, Ireland a Social and Cultural History, London, p. 53.
55. Ernest Blythe, *The State and the Language, An English version of the Presidential address of Ernest Blythe to Comhdháil Náisiúnta na Gaeilge, 3 December, 1949,* 2nd ed., Dublin, Comhdháil Náisiúnta, 1951, p. 193.
56. *Ibid.*
57. *Raucle Tongue, The II.*
58. Roderick Watson, "MacDiarmid and International Modernism", in Scott Lyall & Margery Palmer McCulloch, (eds.), *The Edinburgh Companion to Hugh MacDiarmid,* Edinburgh University Press, 2011, p. 21.
59. *Raucle Tongue, The III*, p. 65.
60. W. A. Craigie, John Buchan, Peter Giles & J. M. Bulloch, *The Scottish Tongue,* London, Toronto & Melbourne, Cassell & Co., 1924.
61. *Modernism and Nationalism* p. 21.
62. *Ibid.*
63. W. A. Craigie, "The Present State of the Scottish Tongue" in W. A. Craigie, John Buchan, Peter Giles & J. M. Bulloch, *The Scottish Tongue,* London, Toronto & Melbourne, Cassell & Co., 1924, pp. 3–46.
64. *MacDiarmid. Christopher Murray Grieve. A Critical Biography*, 1988, p. 129.
65. *Ibid.*, p. 137.
66. "'Satori' in Scotland" in Miller, (ed.), (1970), p. 58.
67. *Scottish Biographies 1938,* pub; by E; J; Thurston, London, Jackson, Son & Co; Ltd., Glasgow, p. 781. In the same volume his friend, Nannie K. Wells, said that her hobby was, "managing rheumaticky minds with modern electric shock treatment." Scottish nationalists were capable of making jokes.
68. As was recognised by H. J. Paton, *The Claim of Scotland*, Aberdeen University Press, 1968, p. 270.
69. *The Flag in the Wind*, p. 35.
70. The only non-Scot to make the accusation was Gwynfor Evans, the Welsh nationalist leader, and he too did not quote specific remarks. See Gwynfor Evans *For the Sake of Wales the Memoirs of Gwynfor Evans*, translated from the Welsh by Meic Stephens, Cardiff, Welsh Academic Press, 1996, p. 60.
71. He was a Fellow of the Royal Anthropological Institute.
72. Lewis Spence, *Freedom for Scotland. The Case for Scottish Self-Government,* Edinburgh, The Scottish National Movement, n.d. [1927], p. 6.
73. *The Standard* March 1922.

74. *Edinburgh Evening News*, 2nd January 1922.
75. *Edinburgh Evening News*, 2nd January 1922.
76. *Ibid.*, 13ᵗʰ January 1922.
77. London, T. Fisher Unwin, Ltd., 1920, pp. 142–3.
78. *Ibid.*, p. 5.
79. *Ibid.*, p. 143.
80. Willa Muir *Belonging a Memoir* London, The Hogarth Press, 1968, p. 116.
81. *Raucle Tongue, The III*, p. 457.
82. "'Satori' in Scotland", in Karl Miller, (ed.), *Memoirs of a Modern Scotland,* London, Faber & Faber, 1970, p. 57.
83. *Albyn* p. 78.
84. *Albyn* p. 81.
85. *Raucle Tongue, The III*, p. 203.
86. *Ibid.,* p. 205.

4

Red

MacDiarmid and Communism

The waves of their purposefulness go flooding through me.
This religion is simple, naked. Its claims stand out
In black and white. It is the wind of God;
Like standing on a mountaintop in a gale
Binding, compelling yet gloriously freeing.
It contains nothing tawdry or trivial.
In its very ugliness it is compelling,
Its bleakness uplifting.
It holds me in a fastness of security.

("The Covenanters" from *Second Hymn
to Lenin and Other Poems*.)[1]

MacDiarmid's Communism might imply that he had surrendered his independence of mind. According to Neal Wood, intellectuals who were members of the British Communist Party were under constant pressure to set aside critical thought.[2] MacDiarmid's statement, in 1932, that he was, "an orthodox Communist, subscribing without any hesitation or qualification to Moscow direction"[3] might be taken as evidence of this but, in fact, he was not a member of the Party at that time. When he did join, his deviations proved to be more than the Party could tolerate. He was a Communist by *his* definition and on *his* terms.

He did not become a communist as a result of his encounter with militant class struggle in South Wales. In fact, as we have seen, he detoured through right wing ideas before he joined the Communist Party of Great Britain in 1934. He did so after reconnecting with his working class origins through an imaginative return to the Langholm of his youth. His purpose was not to promote international class struggle, but to support the USSR as a liberator of small nations, his priority remained Scottish independence. He was a highly unorthodox Communist, but he did make an original contribution to Marxist thought about Scotland.

Backward *Forward*

His admiration for the USSR began in 1928. This was the year of
the formation of the National Party of Scotland and the NPS put up
candidates against the London-based parties, including Labour. In
response the Labour newspaper *Forward* published a number of articles
criticising the nationalists. One of the writers was the veteran socialist
propagandist John S. Clarke.[4] He alleged that nationalism had led to ten
million deaths between 1914 and 1918, but now,

> Capitalism ... is spreading a uniform culture or technique
> throughout the world. Man to man the world o'er shall brothers
> be, as the poet foresaw over a century ago. The propaganda of
> Nationalism, were it effective, would retard the day of human
> brotherhood. A man cannot nourish national vanity without
> nourishing a contempt for men of other nations.[5]

He challenged the concept of a national culture and denied the existence
of Scottish art. Raeburn, he argued, was not a Scottish artist just
because he painted "a man in kilts", he had painted "Scottish ladies and
gentlemen using the technique which universal art in its evolution had
perfected."[6]

MacDiarmid detested this kind of abstract internationalism and he
attacked Clarke's use of a superficial knowledge of art and literature to
impress the working class readers of *Forward,* while doing nothing to
raise their cultural level.

> The ... organ of the Movement claiming to be for the uplift of the
> masses ... panders as brazenly to the mob as any "Capitalist rag"
> and serves up a hideous mixture of Socialist and Labour politics,
> mid-Victorianism, cheap personalia, slang, patent medicine
> advertisements and what not, with ... a queer compound of
> Calvinism, Total Abstinence, and the Musical Festival Movement,
> by way of an adumbration of the Future Culture of Our People.[7]

He went on to outline what a "saner socialism" would have to say about
arts and culture. They should be the free heritage of all humanity, but
they had been monopolised by the privileged classes:

> These things are good – they represent the ends to which everything
> else in life should be merely the means.... And just there this
> saner Socialism encounters its principal snag.... Everything of

value in the world has been – and will remain – the creation of
a few; and must be constantly recreated by the few, frequently in
the face of the opposition, and nearly always of the apathy and
indifference, of the masses who ultimately benefit.[8]

MacDiarmid believed that society should spread its cultural benefits
as widely as possible but, in the meantime, arts and literature should
be preserved by an elite, and not diluted for the sake of popular tastes.
This led to a dual strategy, a revival of Scottish culture and a socialism
that did not resort to meaningless internationalist rhetoric. He thought
he saw a model for this in nationalities policy of the Soviet Union.

Leninism

He cited Stalin's *Leninism* which,

> ... brings out clearly how within the USSR itself nationalisms,
> suppressed under Tsarist imperialism, have sprung into new life.
> Post-Revolution Russian literature is by far the most intensely
> nationalist in Europe today – perhaps the most nationalistic the
> world has ever seen."[9]

Leninism was a collection of Stalin's essays and speeches, which had
been published in an English translation in 1928. MacDiarmid must
have noticed the following, from a speech made while the Stalin was
Soviet Commissar of Nationalities:

> The socialist revolution far from cutting down the number of
> languages ... has actually increased the number, for, by arousing
> the broad masses of humanity, by leading them to take an interest
> in political life, socialism has stirred up a veritable hive of hitherto
> unknown or quasi-unknown nationalities. Who ever realised that
> Tsarist Russia harboured no fewer than fifty nationalities and
> ethnic groups within its borders?[10]

MacDiarmid read this as a declaration of the rights of small nations
and it is true that the Soviet government promoted minority languages
and cultures in its early years, giving some of them a written form for
the first time. But Stalin reversed this policy when nationalists in the
Ukraine resisted the drive to collectivise agriculture[11] and the Soviet
government then sought to Russify the smaller republics.[12] However,

in 1928, Stalin's book persuaded MacDiarmid that socialism and nationalism could be reconciled through Soviet Communism.

There were other factors at work, he lost his battle to stay in the NPS and his *Albyn* strategy fell apart. The Crofter agitation on Lewis had not proved to be a prelude to wider agitation, in fact land raiding diminished significantly[13] and the Highland Land League merged with the Labour Party. The Red Clydesiders did not become nationalists, the Scottish economy enjoyed a boom because of post-war reconstruction, so that the Scottish Labour Movement emerged from the First World War in a better political and organisational position than in the rest of the UK. This was what had led to a short-lived upsurge of interest in Home Rule,[14] but once the post-war depression had taken hold, Labour reverted to Unionism.[15]

The "Irish Invasion" was going into reverse, the 1931 census showed that there were almost 34,724 fewer Irish in Scotland than in 1921.[16] And the leaders of the Irish community were not interested in "re-Gaelicising" Scotland, they "... were more concerned with material advancement or simple survival than with sorting out their relationship with the Scottish nation and the Labour Party was the obvious vehicle for them."[17] The anti-Irish statements of a small number of prominent nationalists made Labour, and Westminster, seem a better bet than an Edinburgh parliament with a Presbyterian majority.

The NPS was not been won over to Social Credit. In fact, support waned once the Major's "Plan for Scotland" came under critical scrutiny. When the Social Credit Party of Scotland was formed in 1935, Douglasites and Scottish Nationalists became electoral competitors and this ended any prospect of a political alliance.

This New Civilisation

A key moment in MacDiarmid's move towards communism came in February 1933, when he described the Soviet Union as "this new civilisation".[18] The phrase is reminiscent of Sidney and Beatrice Webb's, *Soviet Communism a New Civilisation*, but that book did not appear until 1935. What had influenced him was Robert Briffault's, *Breakdown. The Collapse of Traditional Civilisation,* published in 1932. Briffault was a popular writer on anthropology and he rejected Marxism. But, anticipating the Webbs, he noticed the new developments in the USSR during the early 1930s.

The first Five Year Plan had ended in 1932 and had, "undeniably been a success in its Bolshevik aims ..."[19] Stalin's leadership had been consolidated, but the Terror and the show trials had not yet begun.

There had been widespread collectivisation of agriculture, with some introduction of modern farming methods. Production of coal, oil, iron and steel had been boosted. Factories, power stations and railroads were being built. This was the heroic era of Soviet construction and ambitious claims were being made about the building of socialism in one country. Observed from a distance, the human costs could be overlooked and Briffault declared,

> For the first time in history the organisation of a human society has been undertaken – with a view to organising, not exploiting. For the first time in history the antique tradition which licensed robbery by private individuals ... has been uncompromisingly and utterly disregarded. The event was at first spoken of as anarchy. Later it was referred to as terror. It is now sometimes spoken of as an experiment.[20]

MacDiarmid quoted a key passage:

> We are engaged upon the lunatic occupation of trying to run the world in terms of things and values that no longer exist as a belief in any human soul.... the idea that a profiteer chaos can be mended by our rulers ... is the most ludicrous imbecility. Of the two alternative issues to our present situation – a decent effort towards veracity or the deluge – we need have no expectation whatever of the former. The Bolsheviks, not the Profiteers, will win because they have the motive power, belief in their ideals, which our profiteer civilisation has not.[21]

Briffault's phrase, "profiteer chaos", paralleled Social Credit and he resembled Spengler in his cyclical view of human history, which led him to predict the imminent collapse of Western civilisation and the ascendancy of the USSR. Briffault's book meshed with a number of MacDiarmid's existing ideas and it provided him with another stepping stone to the Communist movement.

Class Against Class

In 1933 MacDiarmid was described as a member of "the British Section of the Revolutionary Writers of the World, a Communist body controlled from Moscow".[22] This must have referred to the International Union of Revolutionary Writers, which was set up in 1930 and was superseded in 1934 by the Writers International. This was the first time he had declared a Communist affiliation and he was officially accepted into membership of the Communist Party itself in the summer of 1934.[23]

Most of the intellectuals who embraced communism in the 1930s did so because they believed that the USSR and international Communism were the only forces strong enough to check Nazi Germany and Fascist Italy. The 1930s intellectuals expressed, in Stephen Spender's words, "the problem of the liberal divided between his individual development and his social conscience."[24] But MacDiarmid was not a liberal, he did not have a divided soul, and he was not wracked by Spender's guilt about having been born into a privileged social status.[25]

Another crucial difference was that he became a Communist before most of the 1930s intake, in fact he did so during the "Third Period", when the Communist International was actively repelling any liberals who attempted to climb on board.

> ...the Comintern posited a "third period" in revolutionary development...as the world entered a period of renewed breakdown...the appropriate response for Communist parties was to adopt a stance of "class against class"...and combat the social democratic misleaders and their parties...[26]

The Communists not only opposed the bourgeois parties, they labelled the moderate socialists "social fascists" and at times gave a higher priority to opposing the leaders of reformist working class movements than to fighting fascism. The few writers, artists or academics who did join were considered to have "no special role in their own intellectual fields, or in winning the majority of their own social groups to the socialist cause."[27] MacDiarmid's future political development was influenced by the time at which he joined the Party. That was why his rhetoric was more extreme than that of other Communist intellectuals. And his lack of middle-class guilt made him more willing to challenge the Party leadership, particularly when he developed his own Marxist analysis of Scotland.

Arrant Idealism

The veteran Scottish Nationalist Archie Lamont discussed MacDiarmid's Marxism in an illuminating way, it was based neither on *Capital* nor on Marx's theories about surplus value, but it was akin to the *Theses on Feuerbach:*

> For Descartes' formula *I think* Feuerbach substituted *I am and I think,* giving the precedence to Being and making Thought

a secondary consideration. This was the opposite of Hegel who regarded Thought as creative and primary. Marx and Engels followed Feuerbach and regarded Being and Thought as inseparable. Being, however, was the subject controlling the object, Thought. For Marx *I Am* plus *I Think* produces the Idea that is capable of changing the environment. This is indeed very like a return to the idealist position in which Thought has precedence.[28]

MacDiarmid did not imbibe his Marxism from Party sources, he had, after all, first encountered Marxist ideas before the Russian Revolution. But even taking this into account, his Marxism looks distinctly odd. He never expressed a belief in class struggle as the driving force of human development nor that individuals are the products of their social and economic circumstances. He rarely quoted from the Marxist classics, and when he did so it was usually at second hand. He did not depict industrial workers as the most important progressive force in society, nor did he laud the struggles of working class communities.

He was, in any case, primarily interested in the aesthetics of Marxism, not in its political and economic theories. Neal Ascherson makes the perceptive point that,

> ... it was the colossal scale of the Marxist theory which appealed to him, the way in which – especially in the hands of Engels – all of the universe, its gas, its floating scintillas of shattered planets, its human beings, its stones were related in one solemn music. It was the cosmology in all its boldness and comprehensiveness which drew him.[29]

MacDiarmid was a poet and Marxism was a stimulus to his imagination. He was not tied to a narrowly political interpretation and his mind constantly tried to encompass conflicting intellectual systems. In 1952 he defended his Marxism in a letter to the American scholar Edith Trelease Aney,

> You ask about the apparent incompatibility of some of my views with Communism, or at least with the line enforced in the USSR. I think 'apparent' is the operative word. As Engels pointed out he and Marx had only been able to do about a third of what they had planned. Amongst other things they had failed to implement their philosophy with an aesthetic....[30]

His claim was that Marx and Engels had not contributed significantly to an understanding of art and literature. Later Marxists, like Gramsci and

Lukács, did extend Marxism in this direction, but their writings became influential only after MacDiarmid had formed his own interpretation.

Another source of his unorthodoxy was his encounter with the writings of American philosopher Sidney Hook,[31] who argued that Hegel had been far more significant in the formation of Marx's ideas than most Marxists had understood.[32] Hook was an independent Marxist thinker who was, at that time, close to Trotskyism.[33] If MacDiarmid was aware of the American's heretical status, he was unconcerned. He showed an intuitive grasp of his ideas, in particular his explanation of Hegel's dialectic as a method of critical thought.

This made his Marxism unrecognisable to many of his comrades. Many years later David Craig identified their problem when he criticised the following lines from MacDiarmid's "Third Hymn to Lenin":

> ... only one or two in every million men today
> Know that thought is reality – and thought alone!

They displayed, Craig alleged,

> ... the most arrant idealism – treating the mental processes that depend on material existence as somehow higher than it, 'more real'. It is what the great thinkers in the Marxist-Leninist tradition have fought against time and time again."[34]

Craig's critique reflected what the Communist Party then understood as Marxist philosophy. It claimed that there was a profound gulf between "materialist" and "idealist" views of reality, as a CPGB text book put it,

> Idealism is the way of interpreting things which regards the spiritual as prior to the material, whereas materialism regards the material as prior. Idealism supposes that everything material is dependent on and determined by something spiritual, whereas materialism recognises that everything spiritual is dependent on and determined by something material. And this difference manifests itself both in general philosophical conceptions of the world as a whole, and in conceptions of particular things and events.[35]

If this really was the only legitimate version of Marxism, it would be hard to acquit MacDiarmid of deviation. However, the subsequent lines from the "Third Hymn" offer an insight into his ideas:

> And must absorb all the material – their goal
> The mastery by the spirit of all the facts that can be known.[36]

MacDiarmid was saying that only thought could integrate, into a coherent whole, the vast quantities of knowledge that had been made available by science. He claimed that he was a "a materialist and an atheist" because he believed that, "only a very small portion of reality is accessible to the human mind."[37] But on becoming a Marxist the phenomena he had previously regarded as spiritual he now saw as aspects of material existence which had yet to be explained by science. And whereas he had previously called the ultimate reality "God", he now he called it "matter".

His ideas had some similarity to those of György Lukács who, in his *History and Class Consciousness*, criticised the orthodox Marxism of the late nineteenth century and reasserted the Hegelian content of Marx's thought.

> He set out to show that the chief philosophical disputes among the Marxists of the Second International had been conducted from positions alien to Marx's ideas and, in particular that the orthodox line had continued to ignore the essential feature of dialectical materialism namely the interaction of object and subject in history towards unity.[38]

According to Lukács, Marx had meant that reality could only be apprehended through a process in which subjective thought and objective reality came into a conflict, which was then resolved through action to change the world. On this reading, the Communists had missed Marx's point when they made a rigid dichotomy between thought and matter. Reality consisted of matter and thought in a mutually evolving unity.

The John MacLean Line

MacDiarmid broke Party discipline by standing, without Party permission, for the Rectorship of Edinburgh University in 1935 and 1936. He was the candidate of a "united front of Communists Socialists and Scottish Nationalists"[39] and got the support of a group of young radicals who became the "Red Scotland" group. With them he developed a Marxist critique of the Communist Party's line on Scotland.

In October 1936 he wrote:

> ... far more exacting dialectical discrimination must be given to the alleged consequences of the identity of interests of Scottish and English workers, since this in no wise conflicts with the question of Scottish Independence nor necessarily involves any incorporating

Union of the two peoples, as Marx (and subsequently Lenin) instilled: 'No nation that enslaves another can itself be free.' The freeing of Scotland should be a foremost plank in the programme of the English workers themselves – in their own no less than in Scotland's interest.[40]

MacDiarmid challenged the contradictions in the Communist Party's ideas about Scotland. It had selected certain factors that Scotland and England had in common, particularly factory-based class struggle and working class economic grievances, and had declared them to be primary. It then treated other aspects of Scotland as if they were unreal – its culture, its historical experiences, the folk memory of its people, its sense of nationality. Even consideration of these specifically Scottish phenomena was regarded as inimical to working class unity.

In this way the complexities of Scotland and the significance of its differences with England were ejected from the orbit of Marxist enquiry. Hook had explained that,

> For Marx as for Hegel the social system constitutes a whole. Its various cultural aspects, – educational system, religion, art – are parts of the whole. The real character of any of these aspects cannot be grasped when we isolate it from the context of tradition and living energies which define the culture of an age."[41]

MacDiarmid was trying to break through the barrier caused by the Communist Party's assumption that what it identified as the interests of the British working class must always trump the national interests of Scotland. He criticised the Party for ignoring the cultural reality within which the class struggle took place. This approach had to be eliminated by achieving a deeper and more detailed understanding of Scottish history, society and culture.

In 1936 he issued his "Red Scotland Thesis", in which he tried to persuade the Communist Party that, "the majority of nationalists outside the National Party are left wing socialists and Communists and people sympathetic too and inclined towards Communism." He claimed that the "bourgeois manoeuvre" of the merger between the NPS and the Scottish Party would have been defeated if the Communist Party had "thrown its weight in the scale … ." But they still had "the game in their hands any time they care to play it."[42]

The "game" was a left nationalist line, inspired by the writings of the Glasgow Marxist John MacLean and James Connolly, the Edinburgh born Irish socialist and martyr of the 1916 Rising in Dublin. MacLean had been one of the best known leaders of Red Clydeside, but he refused to join the CPGB, instead he advocated an independent revolutionary party for Scotland. Walter Kendall summarised his ideas:

> MacLean's strategical view formed a unified whole. Scotland dominated by the industrial heartland of the Clyde valley was nearer to socialism than England. Glasgow then should strike the first blow and London would follow, just as Petrograd had begun in Russia.... Scotland was by culture, history and tradition a separate nation. The revolution then must begin with the formation of a specifically Scottish Communist Party which would initiate the Scots revolution and set off the powder train in the rest of Britain.[43]

In 1920 MacLean issued a leaflet headed "All Hail the Scottish Communist Republic!" and in 1923 he founded the Scottish Workers Republican Party. When the leaflet was republished as an election address in 1922 its heading showed the influence of James Connolly, "All Hail the Scottish Workers Republic!"

> ... Scotland must again have independence, but not to be ruled over by traitor chiefs and politicians. The communism of the clans must be re-established on a modern basis. (Bolshevism, to put it roughly, is but the modern expression of the communism of the *mir*.) Scotland must therefore work itself into a communism embracing the whole country as a unit. The country must have but one clan, as it were – a united people working in co-operation and co-operatively, using the wealth that is created.[44]

MacLean added, "We can safely say, then: back to communism and forward to communism." He reminded the Irish in Scotland that "communism prevailed amongst the Irish clans ... "[45], so that by allying with Scottish socialist republicans they would be "carrying forward the traditions and instincts of the Celtic race."

MacDiarmid may have read MacLean's writings before the First World War, and probably heard him speak, but he would have encountered him as an orthodox Marxist who was mainly concerned with economic matters and the two never met, (the "MacLean" referred to in a letter to Ogilvie was the ILP leader Neil MacLean).[46] He did meet some of James Connolly's former comrades in Edinburgh and read some of the Irish socialist's writings. But when he reviewed Desmond Ryan's *James Connolly* in 1924 he saw in it evidence that contradicted Marxism,

> Somehow or other he divined that Socialism and Nationalism must come to terms – that the Marxian dispensation would not answer

the needs of humanity – and his conjunction of revolutionary Socialism and rebel Nationalism was a reflection of the unexpended evolutionary momentum with which the philosophy of Bakunin is steadily undermining the bases of Marxism.[47]

Celtic Communism

Raymond J. Ross traced MacDiarmid's belated interest in MacLean to a biographical pamphlet by the Glasgow Anarchist Guy Aldred, published in 1932. The ILP leader Jimmy Maxton then put MacDiarmid in touch with MacLean's daughter Nan Mercer (later Nan Milton), who gave him copies of her father's writings.[48] This was the basis for his "John MacLean line". He quoted from an election address of MacLean's:

> Scotland's wisest policy is to declare for a Republic in Scotland … The social revolution is possible sooner in Scotland than in England. The working class policy ought to be to break up the Empire to avert war and enable the workers to triumph in every country and colony. Scottish separation is part of the process of England's Imperial disintegration and is a help towards the ultimate triumph of the workers of the world.[49]

This, MacDiarmid wrote, was still relevant, "the secession of Scotland will be one of the deadliest possible blows that can be struck at English Imperialism – a blow at the very heart of the Empire.[50] "We are convinced," he wrote,

> … just as Connolly said that in Ireland the social revolution would be incomplete without a nationalist revolution too, so in Scotland here it is clear that the objectives of the social revolution can only be fully realised if it is accompanied by autonomy on a Communist basis.[51]

His thinking was summed up in a *Voice of Scotland* editorial of 1938. The "tempo and direction of development" of the English and Scottish working class movements was different, as a consequence of the "unequal development" of the capitalist systems in the two countries:

> It is this basic fact that is at the root of the recurrence of the constitutional issues and problems of prestige that bother the nationalists. But it must be remembered that to call the

constitutional problems secondary problems is *not to declare them spurious questions.* Their solution is as vital as that of the underlying economic problems and ultimately cannot be divorced from that task.... *a point must come,* according to MacLean's thesis, at which the relations of Scotland to England must not merely hamper gravely ... but at last absolutely bar ... the onrush of the Scots workers ... This is the point at which Scotland must reassert its nationhood by reclaiming its right of self-determination ... and of setting up a *Scottish Workers' Republic, as destined to be of lasting worth in itself and a factor in the destruction of English imperialism.*[52]

Firm Marxist Bounds

MacDiarmid's version of Scottish Workers' Republicanism was not a revival of the ideas of Connolly and MacLean, which had been ignored or forgotten. It was his own synthesis, put together in the 1930s on the basis of highly selective evidence. It is true that Connolly, influenced by the historian Alice Stopford Green, had attributed the rise of capitalism in Ireland to the Norman invasion, which had overthrown the ancient Celtic forms of communal property, but this can be interpreted as a propaganda point. Anti-socialists were claiming that socialism was a foreign importation and he wanted to prove that it was more native than capitalism. According to David Lynch, although he was trying to "Hibernicise" socialist ideas, Connolly,

> ... believed that there could be no return to the ancient form of 'Celtic communism' ... capitalism would have developed in Ireland eventually with or without a Norman invasion. The future socialist society would be a 'reorganisation of society on the basis of a broader and more developed form of that common property which underlay the social structure of Ancient Erin'.[53]

James D, Young analysed MacLean's writings and concluded that, although he did endorse Scottish independence, his strategy was based on the uneven development of the working class movements in Scotland and England, not on the principle of Scottish autonomy and he had "kept his proud nationalism within firm Marxist bounds"[54] And Iain McLean suggests that, because MacLean believed there would be a war between the rival imperialisms of Britain and America, he saw a successful Scottish revolution as a means of stopping the Clyde from being used as a strategic location in this conflict.[55]

MacLean did collaborate, albeit briefly, with Scottish nationalists[56] and he did support Scottish self-government. But he clearly distinguished between the programme of the nationalists and his own, class-based, strategy,

> Scotland, however, can only have real independence for all her inhabitants under communism controlled and evolved by workers' committees as in Russia … The old communal traditions of the clans must be revived and adapted to modern conceptions and conditions. If the Bolshevik notion of world communism through national communism is scientifically correct then we are justified in using our latent Highland and Scottish sentiments in the mighty task confronting us of transforming capitalism into communism.[57]

He had used Erskine of Mar's writings for the purposes of socialist propaganda, but a former comrade, James MacDougall, argued that MacLean's nationalism was not just a temporary tactic or aberration. There had been a "curious sub-conscious Scottish effect", he wrote, in the intransigence of the pre-1917 left-wing Marxists in Scotland. And Lenin's stance on self-determination for small nations had influenced Maclean and his Scottish Workers Republican Party.[58] This is implies a subtle influence on MacLean's thought, which made him more willing to work with nationalists than most other Scottish Marxists, but it does not validate MacDiarmid's interpretation. MacLean, like Connolly, used ideas about communal ownership in ancient Celtic society to make propaganda for modern socialist ideas. His support for a separate Scottish Communist Party and his call for a "Workers' Republic" seem to have been conjunctural and not a matter of fixed principle.

MacDiarmid originally emphasised MacLean's idea that Scotland was a weak link in the chain of British imperialism, but in later years he presented him as an exemplar of Scotland's Gaelic heritage.

> MacLean came at the end of a long sequence of Scottish radical and republican thinkers, that this doctrine is, as Rudolf Bringhamm [*sic*], William Ferris and other writers on the Gaelic Commonwealth show, a doctrine profoundly related to our hidden Gaelic traditions.…[59]

In fact, Ferris was profoundly anti-socialist and wanted a restoration of the ancient Celtic monarchy, not a Workers' Republic. Rudolf Bringmann was a minor scholar who wrote a history of Ireland for German readers, published in Berlin in 1939.[60] His book was based on existing Irish sources and said nothing original. He has been identified as a "Nazi sympathiser"[61] and, at the very least, he had adapted to the Third Reich. He was even less appropriate than Ferris as an authority for MacDiarmid's claims.

Oppressed Nations

The Communist International was more ambiguous about nationalism than MacDiarmid recognised. In *Red Scotland* he referred to the theses on the "National and Colonial Questions" that Lenin had drafted for the Second Congress of the Comintern in 1920. The fourth thesis had declared,

> ... the policy of the Communist International on national and colonial questions must be chiefly to bring about a union of the proletarian and working masses for a joint revolutionary struggle leading to the overthrow of capitalism, through which national inequality and oppression can be abolished.[62]

However, the second thesis qualified this support for nationalism. Communists should distinguish "the interests of the oppressed classes of the workers and the exploited, from the general concept of so-called national interests, which signify in fact the interests of the ruling class". They should also distinguish between "the oppressed, dependent nations" and "the oppressing, exploiting nations."[63]

The Comintern assumed that national movements which were worthy of Communist support would have a social base in the peasantry. As Stalin wrote," ... the ruling nationality exploits and oppresses the masses, and above all the peasant masses, of the colonies and dependencies, and ... the imperialists spur them on to the struggle against imperialism, and make them the allies of the proletarian revolution.[64] The Comintern's tactic was to use national grievances to get the peasants into a united front with the working class to overthrow capitalist imperialism. National liberation might be a by-product, but if it got in the way of the advancing proletariat it would be jettisoned.

Ireland was regarded as an oppressed nation and there was a long tradition of Marxist support for Irish resistance to British rule, originating with Marx and Engels. This was based on the belief that the main engine of social revolution in Ireland was the struggle of tenant farmers against the landlords. The Comintern overlooked the fact that in 1903 the Irish land question had been, for the most part, solved by British legislation.[65] Scotland, on the other hand, was seen as an industrialised society whose remaining land grievances were not important. Scotland

and Ireland fell on different sides of the Comintern's dividing line, and MacDiarmid found himself working against the grain of both the Comintern and the CPGB.

The Popular Front

Harry McShane, a contemporary of Connolly and MacLean, remembered that he and his Scottish CPGB comrades had derided MacLean's "socialism in kilts" in the 1920s and, in the 1930s, they saw the demand for Scottish self-government as a reversion to the radical liberalism of the late 19th century.[66] Like most Scottish Communists they thought that, "the whole National Agitation was an artificially fostered thing designed simply to provide jobs for certain middle class people."[67] But they did not deny their national identity, on the contrary no Communist social occasion was complete without recitations and songs from Robert Burns. An Icelandic scholar commented on the paradox in their attitudes:

> On the one hand we have an attempt to combine Communist rhetoric and ideology with Scottish national sentiment and Scottish cultural, if not political traditions ... On the other hand we find a complete rejection of any such attempts on the rounds that harnessing Scottish nationalist aspirations would diminish British as well as international, working class solidarity.[68]

This was an attitude that had been carried into the Communist Party from early twentieth century socialists like John S. Clark, who saw agitation on national and cultural questions as a diversion from the economic class struggle.

Not all Scottish Communists dismissed self-government completely. Before MacDiarmid joined the Party one of its key women leaders, Helen Crawfurd, had offered a closely reasoned argument that Scotland did suffer economic disadvantages within the Union. She did not advocate Home Rule, but she cited Engels' and Lenin's view that federation would be a progressive step for the United Kingdom.[69] However, during the rigidities of the Third Period, her arguments made no impression on the Party.

This phase came to an end in 1935, when the Seventh Congress of the Comintern laid down its new Popular Front strategy. The Nazi revolution in Germany had smashed the Communist Party of Germany, which had been the most powerful outside the USSR. This directly threatened the Soviet Union and the Comintern's new priority was the unity of all opponents of fascism, including middle class liberals and democratic nationalists. The Popular Front was meant to bring the workers together with the "toiling peasants, the urban petty bourgeoisie and the toiling masses of the oppressed nationalities". It would also defend the rights of "progressive intellectuals" and "give them every support in their movement against cultural reaction."[70] In other words it was supposed to incorporate most of the forces MacDiarmid had hailed in *Albyn,* as the basis for a national revival in Scotland. This was an opportunity for him to present his *Red Scotland* line as consistent with the strategy of the international Communist movement.

Questions of Freedom

This made a change of attitude towards the national question in Scotland seem possible. In 1935 Tom Wintringham noted, in the Communist literary journal *Left Review,* that Scottish and Welsh writers had posed, "questions of freedom that we must answer."[71] But a special Scottish number, published just over a year later, produced new grounds for rejecting a nationalist line. An editorial stated that,

> It is of the first importance that any movements in defence of regional or national cultures should develop in a progressive rather than a reactionary sense. We have therefore devoted a large part of this number to a discussion of Scottish problems, in the hope of throwing some light on the question of how far an independent cultural tradition can be used in the fight against Imperialism, and how far the concept of nationalism is today purely romantic.[72]

The writer was the novelist James Barke, a Party sympathiser. He claimed that only a small section of the middle class intelligentsia felt any sense of national injustice. Scottish nationalism had been promoted by Fleet Street as part of a circulation war, the result was that, "much strength which ought to accrue to the Left in Scotland is actually diverted into reactionary channels."[73] The Scottish people did have a sense of national pride and it had traditions of fighting for freedom and of social progress, but this was the heritage of the workers and peasants, who were "the class in whose hands the future lies."[74] Writers and intellectuals had to ally themselves with the working class if they were to realise their humanitarian and anti-fascist aspirations.

In a review of Stalin's, *Marxism and the National and Colonial Question* Edgell Rickword, the editor of *Left Review,* raised another barrier against MacDiarmid's strategy,

... a local nationalism not based on a realisation of the class struggle is the attempt of the middle class sections whose existence becomes more and more threatened by monopoly-capitalism to preserve themselves. But as the examples of Germany and Italy show, the developments towards war and Fascism makes hay of their class and individual interests.... It is only through participation in the working-class-democratic struggle that the national characteristics can revive and flourish ...[75]

Barke and Rickword assumed that all intellectuals were middle class and that they had to ally with the working class if they wanted to contribute to the struggle against fascism. Since the gatekeeper to the workers was the Communist Party, intellectuals had to accept the Party line and campaign under the directions of its leadership. If many of these Party leaders happened to be narrow minded philistines, that was just one more flail with which privileged intellectuals were expected to scourge themselves. "Class first nation second,"[76] Barke insisted, and he recognised no middle ground between the working class, led by the Communist Party, and fascism.

Consideration of Scottish independence was excluded at the outset, and it was further prejudged by asking Neil M. Gunn to defend the nationalist case. He poked gentle fun at the Communist Party's historical and philosophical arguments, but he argued in explicitly non-Marxist terms and this meant that MacDiarmid's case for a nationalist line in Scotland was ignored. MacDiarmid was bitter, noting that he had been excluded from the pages of the Scottish number, even though he was the only Scottish writer who was actually a member of the Party, and despite the fact that Tom Wintringham had named him as one of those who had posed "questions of freedom". It should have been a turning point, MacDiarmid wrote, but it had been in the wrong hands,

> The result was that the issue was hopelessly confused and weak, and that the realignment in Communist Party policy in relation to Scotland, which it should have heralded, did not take place for another couple of years, and, when it did take place, had the same weaknesses as this special issue itself....[77]

Unfortunately for MacDiarmid the Party was not "confused and weak", it was dogmatically certain and he was unable to breach the walls it had erected against original thought and argument on the national question in Scotland.

Continual War with England

MacDiarmid attempted to use the example of the French Popular Front. The anti-fascist coalition government in Paris had a defence pact with the USSR, there was a mass French Communist Party and a long established working class movement. France had an historic antagonism with Germany and it faced an internal threat from the extreme right. James F, McMillan describes how the "Communists went to enormous lengths to project a favourable image of themselves as a truly French and patriotic party". The leader of the Party, Maurice Thorez, declared that, they were "reconciling the tricolour of their fathers with the red flag of their hopes", and "... even proffered a hand to French Catholics, which was not, in the event, clasped."[78] He reported to the Comintern that they had retrieved, "... from our enemies the things they had stolen from us and trampled underfoot. We took back the Marseillaise and the Tricolour."[79]

MacDiarmid quoted from Claude Cockburn's periodical *The Week*,

> *The movement is in the direction of the consolidation around the Third International of those who in each country are genuinely 'patriotic' – are genuinely in favour of the defence of 'la Patrie'." – as opposed, for example to ... the ... patriotic leaders who have patriotically' armed Hitler Germany....*[80]

This, however, was a short lived tactical manoeuvre not a change of heart. After the fall of France the Communists refused to support resistance to the German occupation until after the Nazi invasion of the USSR,[81] the priority was to support the foreign policy of the Kremlin and the national interests of France were secondary.

The Glasgow Communist leader Peter Kerrigan attacked MacDiarmid in the *Daily Worker* of 25 November 1935.[82] He had been provoked by "Scotland France and Working Class Interests", which appeared in *New Scotland* of October 1935. MacDiarmid had referred to an article in *Left Review* which predicted that the coming war would see Britain and Germany allied against France and the United States. The threatened war with France should lead to a revival of the "Auld Alliance" of the Scots and the French and MacDiarmid declared that Scotland must secede from the Union and transform the coming war "into a civil war in Great Britain itself.[83] He argued that, "it was impossible to be a Scottish nationalist without breaking with English culture". This was what the French Communists were doing, they were, "not concerned with preserving French civilisation as it has been – but with getting down to French *Ur*-motives, under communism." He concluded by calling for an, " unbreakable alliance with France and continual war with England."[84]

For Kerrigan,

> Such a line as Hugh MacDiarmid develops can only cause the utmost confusion and mislead many sincere Scottish workers who love their country and have a strong feeling of national pride in Scotland's historical struggle during the past centuries in defence of its democratic rights and liberties.[85]

Saving the Scottish people, "from the shackles of decaying monopoly capitalism and from the threat of Fascism ... calls for the closest unity with the English and Welsh workers...." He quoted Stalin's definition of a nation, claiming that it was, "sufficient for a single one of these characteristics to be absent and the nation ceases to be a nation. ... Scotland is not a non-sovereign nation and therefore we cannot put forward the demand for political secession.[86] MacDiarmid's call for a Scottish war of secession, he charged, was a distortion of Communist policy.

> If in spite of the joint efforts of the British workers such an imperialist war took place, our task in Scotland would be, together with the rest of the British workers, to struggle for the proletarian revolution to "avert the destruction of culture, and raise it to its highest stage of flowering as a truly national culture – national in form and socialist in content."[87]

Stalin's formulations were rendered even more mechanical by Kerrigan's dogmatism and MacDiarmid brushed him aside:

> I accept Comrade Stalin's definition of a nation and, that one unsupported statement is as good as another. He says that ... Scotland is not a nation. I say that it is.... Mr. Kerrigan ... shows an incapacity for the very simplest reasoning ... which ... renders it highly unlikely that he is capable of any real perception of the dialectical process....[88]

"The Essence of MacLeanism"

In the Scottish Peace Council book *Eleventh Hour Questions,* MacDiarmid stressed the differences between Scotland and England. Scotland suffered from, "English imperialistic oppression and ... stands at a more advanced stage of capitalist development."[89] The "second industrial revolution in Scotland", with its emphasis on the development of luxury goods in place of traditional industries meant a drift towards corporatism, with the Scottish Economic Advisory Council, the Highland Reconstruction League and other boards. These facts required a distinctly Scottish alliance that would be more left wing and, "more extreme in its opposition to war."[90]

In the same volume, the Communist MP Willie Gallacher stressed the need for collective security, the strengthening of the League of Nations and international sanctions against the aggressive acts of the fascist regimes. He advocated the widest possible united front in Britain to stop rearmament and to nationalise the arms industry.[91] Gallacher, following Comintern policy, wanted an international alliance between states, to defend the USSR, the role of popular mobilisation was to exert pressure on capitalist governments to support this alliance. But, tone deaf to the new line, MacDiarmid was agitating for a revolutionary struggle from below, on the Third Period model that prevailed when he joined the Party.

The article from *Left Review* cited by MacDiarmid had actually corresponded quite closely to the predictions being made by the Comintern about the line up of forces in the coming war. It had declared that Nazi Germany was threatening the USSR in alliance with "fascist Poland", British imperialism was attempting to weaken France and turn Germany eastwards, to create a "counterbalance" to the United States.[92] But the CPGB did not interpret this as a signal to back France against Britain, instead it gave greater urgency to the struggle for unity against fascism at home. The main forces to be attracted into the Popular Front were the trade unions and the Labour Party and, since these were organised on an all-British basis, a nationalist line in Scotland was incompatible with the Party's strategy.

MacDiarmid had quoted the Welsh nationalist leader, Saunders Lewis :

The Welsh working people see now that the English Labour Party and Trade Union Congress are imperialist, pro-capitalist organisations, prepared to go to war in defence of the English Empire. Welsh nationalism is the Welsh working people's only defence against English militarism.[93]

Kerrigan was outraged by MacDiarmid's comment that Scottish workers should come to similar conclusions.

The attitude of Hugh MacDiarmid to the "English Labour Party and the Trade Union Congress" is a libel on millions of workers, including hundreds of thousands in Scotland. The support which many leaders in the Trade Union and Labour Movement in England (and Scotland) have given to British imperialism is no reason for condemning the T.U.C. and the Labour Party.[94]

This was another obstacle for MacDiarmid. The abandonment of the "class against class" strategy had boosted the influence of those leaders of British Communism who were closest to the trade unions. For them the Popular Front line answered a deep-rooted psychological need.

Their conviction that the Party had to be anchored firmly inside the trade union movement had been reflexive. They had imbibed trade union loyalism with their first experiences of work and economic conflict, along with every other working class activist of their generation. They were socialised into the article of faith developed by British trade union activists since the 1860s, that a 'good' trade union member was unflinchingly and unquestionably loyal to the 'movement'.[95]

Despite his activity during the General Strike, MacDiarmid had never been accultured into trade unionism. Kerrigan, by contrast, was engineering union veteran and former Commissar of the International Brigade in Spain, who would become the CPGB's Industrial Organiser. He spoke to the mainstream of the Communist Party in a way that MacDiarmid never could.

We Stand For "Scotland a Nation"

MacDiarmid launched his own periodical *The Voice of Scotland*, in the summer of 1938. In the first number he published his "Red Scotland Thesis" and, in an editorial, took issue with Kerrigan:

Whereas Stalin has rightly defined a nation as a group that can point to a community, in matters of economics, geography, language. Psychology, and culture, and the absence of any one of these factors removes any group from the claim to nationality, we unhesitatingly affirm that Scotland is a nation under this definition, despite the fact that it is meantime cheated out of its sovereignty to its own grave detriment, the detriment of the world and, since no nation that enslaves another can be free, the gravest detriment of the workers of the oppressing nation (England) itself ...[96]

As MacDiarmid had noted, the line did change. The CPGB stopped labelling the SNP as fascist and, in *Labour Monthly,* Helen Crawfurd revived her support for Engels' ideas on federal self-government. Another Red Clydeside veteran, Aitken Ferguson, produced a paper for the Scottish Committee which proposed support for a Scottish Parliament. He was the only one to vote for it, but in 1938 the Scottish Committee published his pamphlet *Scotland,* which called for a "new legislative body", with "wide powers" over Scottish taxation and budget and, "to compel reactionary elements to toe the line."[97] Some of Ferguson's rhetoric was stirring,

> We Communists stand four square for the full freedom of Scotland to develop her economy, her cultural heritage, her people.
>
> We stand for the right of the Scottish people to decide for themselves their own destiny.[98]

But there was a catch,

> Just as we stand for "Scotland a Nation", so at the same time we stand for strong centralised organisations of the **British** working class on a democratic basis both for the industrial and the political fight, as an essential condition for countering the intensely centralised forces of Britain's millionaire capitalists.[99]

And the immediate demand made in the pamphlet was not legislative autonomy, it was for a Grand Committee of the Westminster Parliament, composed of all the Scottish MPs, augmented by representatives from town and county councils, meeting in Edinburgh to discuss Scotland's future.[100] MacDiarmid had failed to convince even the most nationally conscious of his comrades to support Scottish independence.

Nationalist Deviations

There seemed to be another opportunity shortly after the outbreak of War. His friend, the Gaelic poet Sorley MacLean, made a significant comment:

> I would not care to say how much MacDiarmid was sustained during these years, 1936 to 1939 by the Communist belief that fascism was just the last kicks of Capitalism and that its triumph would be short-lived; and that therefore one ought not to be greatly concerned with the defence of a rotten pluto-democracy against a

brutal but more short lived kind of Capitalism.... I just do not know how much he accepted the Communist Party line between September 1939 and the Nazi invasion of Russia in June 1941.[101]

This referred to the convolutions of the CPGB between the outbreak of WW2 and the Nazi invasion of the USSR. At first the Party supported the war as a struggle against fascism, but after the Nazi-Soviet pact it denounced the war as imperialist. After Hitler's attack on the USSR the line changed again and the Party called for all-out support for the war effort.

In its anti-war period the Party replaced the Popular front line with a call for a "People's Government", which would get rid of the capitalist politicians and allow the workers to organise their own defence against the Axis powers.[102] And it promoted a "People's Convention" with a six point manifesto: "the defence of the people's living standards, the defence of the people's democratic rights, adequate air raid precautions, friendship with the Soviet Union, the formation of a people's government and a people's peace to end the war."[103]

MacDiarmid seized on this, and he wrote to MacLean,

> ... whereas at the People's Convention meeting in London nothing was said at all about Scottish Independence, despite a strong resolution to that effect from the subordinate Scottish People's Convention, now the London people have been compelled to agree to a considerable measure of Scottish autonomy... and all is now set fair for the establishment of a Scottish People's Convention equal in status to the English body.[104]

However the USSR was invaded before this body could be convened. The line changed for a third time and the Convention strategy was dropped.

Nationalist Deviations

There was no room in the CPGB of the 1930s for someone as individual and outspoken as MacDiarmid, so it is not surprising that he was expelled. He alleged that this was because of "nationalist deviations", but there were more obvious factors, chief amongst these indiscipline. MacDiarmid was publishing *The Voice of Scotland* without permission and without referring its contents for approval. And there was anger when he included an article criticising English members of the International Brigade in Spain. He launched his Rectorial election campaign in Edinburgh University without permission. He attacked the writers Edwin and Willa Muir, who were being wooed by the Party, and he publicly criticised the CPGB for not backing his "John MacLean's line."

He was expelled by the Scottish Secretariat of the Communist Party in November 1936 and his appeal to the Comintern was remitted to the Party Congress of May 1937, which agreed to overturn the expulsion, with the Scottish delegation voting to keep him out. The Scottish Committee then repeated its demand for him to be expelled, because of his continued failure to toe the line. His membership was finally terminated in February 1939 and this time he did not appeal.[105] It took a World War and a Cold War to create the conditions for his return to the Communist Party.

Notes

1. *Collected Poems,* p. 551.
2. Neal Wood, *Communism and British Intellectuals,* London, Gollancz, 1959, p. 223–4.
3. *The Free Man* September 3rd 1932.
4. Cf. Raymond Challinor, *John S. Clarke, Poet, Politician, Lion-Tamer* London, Pluto Press, 1977.
5. *Forward* 24 March 1928.
6. *Ibid.*
7. *Forward* 23rd June 1928.
8. *Raucle Tongue, The II,* pp. 49–50.
9. *Forward* 7th July.
10. J. V. Stalin, *Leninism,* Eden & Cedar Paul, (trans.), London, Modern Books, 2nd impression, 1932, Vol. 1, p. 272.
11. *cf.* Ronald Grigor Suny *The Soviet Experiment. Russia, the USSR and the Successor States,* Oxford University Press, 1998, p. 286.
12. Graham Smith, "Nationalities Policy from Lenin to Gorbachev", in Graham Smith (ed.) *The Nationalities Question in the Soviet Union,* London & New York, Longman, 1990, pp. 6–7.
13. Leah Leneman, *Land Fit for Heroes? Land Settlement in Scotland After World War I,* Aberdeen University Press, 1989, p. 36.
14. Michael Keating and David Bleiman, *Labour and Scottish Nationalism,* London & Basingstoke, MacMillan, 1979, pp. 63–4.
15. *Ibid.,* pp. 107–8.
16. Richard Finlay, *Modern Scotland, 1914–2000,* London, Profile Books, 2004, p. 94.
17. Tom Gallagher, *Glasgow the Uneasy Peace,* Manchester University Press, 1987, p. 177.
18. *Raucle Tongue, The II,* p. 207.
19. Georg von Rauch, *A History of Soviet Russia,* New York, Washington & London, 1972, p. 219.
20. Briffault, Robert, *Breakdown. The Collapse of Traditional Civilisation,* London, Gollancz, 1935, p. 202.
21. *Raucle Tongue, The II,* pp. 207–8.
22. *Raucle Tongue, The II,* p. 205.
23. John Manson, "The Poet and the Party" *Cencrastus no. 65,* n.d.

24. Quoted in Duncan Glen, *Hugh MacDiarmid and the Scottish Renaissance*, Edinburgh & London, W & R Chambers, 1964, p. 140.
25. "Stephen Spender" in Crossman (ed.),*The God That Failed. Six Studies in British Communism,* London, Hamish Hamilton, 1950, *pp. 234–5.*
26. Willie Thompson, *The Good Old Cause, British Communism 1920–1991,* London, Pluto, 1992, p. 44.
27. Jim Fyrth, "Introduction: In the Thirties", in Jim Fyrth (ed.), *Britain, Fascism and the Popular Front* London, Lawrence & Wishart, 1985, p. 10.
28. *The National Weekly,* 21 March 1953.
29. Scott, & Davis, 1980, p. 228.
30. *New Selected Letters*, p. 290.
31. These were first published in *The Modern Quarterly* 1936 and later as his book, *From Hegel to Marx.* I am grateful to Owen Dudley Edwards for drawing them to my attention.
32. *c.f.* Paul Buhle, *Marxism in the United States: Remapping the history of the American Left,* Verso, London, 1987, pp. 166–7.
33. In 1938 Hook began to give priority to opposing totalitarianism and this led him, via the Congress for Cultural Freedom, to becoming a vehement anti-communist in the 1950s *cf.* Christopher Phelps, *Young Sidney Hook, Marxist and Pragmatist,* Ithaca & London, Cornell University Press, 1997, pp.198–233.
34. "MacDiarmid the Marxist Poet," in K. D. Duval & Sydney Goodsir Smith (eds.) *Hugh MacDiarmid a Festschrift,* Edinburgh, K. D. Duval, 1962, p. 96. John Manson points out that this was written by a young man, reflecting what seemed at the time to be an authoritative Communist position, it should not be taken as a reflection of Craig's mature views.
35. Maurice Cornforth, *Dialectical Materialism an Introduction.* Vol.1, London, Lawrence & Wishart, 1952. p. 20.
36. *Collected Poems II,* p. 899.
37. "Metaphysics and Poetry" in *Selected Prose,* pp. 274–5 *& Albyn,* pp. 107–13.
38. Leszek Kołakowski, *Main Currents of Marxism,* Book Three *The Breakdown,* New York & London, W.W. Norton & Co., c2005, p. 994.
39. Letter to Roland Muirhead, NLS Acc. 3721, Box 3, File 42.
40. *Raucle Tongue, The III,* p. 11.
41. *From Hegel to Marx,* p. 63.
42. NLS MS 27035.
43. Walter Kendall, *The Revolutionary Movement in Britain 1900–21. The Origins of British Communism,* London, Weidenfield & Nicholson, 1969, reprinted 1971, p. 286.
44. Nan Milton (ed.) *John MacLean, In the Rapids of Revolution,* pp. 217–8.
45. *Ibid.,* p. 218.
46. *Letters,* p. 12.
47. *Raucle Tongue, The I,* p. 211.
48. *Raucle Tongue, The III,* p. 47.
49. *Ibid.,* pp. 9–10.
50. NLS ms. 27035.
51. *Lucky Poet,* pp. 143–44.
52. *Voice of Scotland,* December 1938- February 1939, p. 12.
53. David Lynch, *Radical Politics in Modern Ireland. The Irish Socialist Republican Party 1896–1904,* Dublin & Portland Oregon, Irish Academic Press, 2005, p. 119.
54. *John MacLean Clydeside Socialist,* Clydeside Press, 1992 p. 181.
55. Iain McLean, *The Legend of Red Clydeside,* Edinburgh, John Donald, 1983, p. 150.
56. Milton, *John MacLean,* pp. 206–7.
57. Nan Milton (ed.) *John MacLean, In the Rapids of Revolution,* London, Alison & Busby, 1978, p. 219.

58. *National Weekly* 27th November 1948.

59. *Raucle Tongue, The III*, pp. 38–9

60. Rudolf Bringmann, *Geschichte Irlands; ein Kampf um die völkische Freiheit*, Berlin, Junker und Dünnhaupt, 1939. Thanks to Kenneth McLuskey for his translation.

61. See Joachim Fischer in *Irish Studies Review*, Vol. 9, No. 2, August 2001, p. 266.

62. Jane Degras, (ed.) *The Communist International 1919–43, Documents,* Vol. I, Frank Cass, London, p. 141.

63. *Ibid.*

64. "Comment on Semich's Article" in *Leninism*, p. 289.

65. See Stephen Howe, *Ireland and Empire,* Oxford University Press, 2000, for a discussion of "colonial" and "neo-colonial interpretations of Ireland.

66. Harry McShane, & Joan Smith, *Harry McShane. No Mean Fighter,* London, Pluto, 1978, 1978, p. 225.

67. Quoted in Ragenheiður Kristjánsdóttir, "Communists and the National Question in Scotland and Iceland, c. 1930 to c. 1940", *The Historical Journal,* Vol. 45, No. 3, 2002, p. 608.

68. *Ibid.,* p. 602.

69. *Ibid.,* p. 610.

70. Jane Degras (ed.) *The Communist International 1919–43, Documents,* London, Oxford University Press, 1965, Vol. III p. 364.

71. T. H. Wintringham, "Who is for Liberty?" Left Review, Vol. 1, No. 2, September 1935.

72. Left Review, Vol. 2, No. 14, November 1936.

73. *Ibid.*, Also in McCulloch, (ed.) Modernism and Nationalism, pp. 367–70.

74. *Ibid.*

75. *Ibid.*

76. Quoted in Gustav H, Klaus, "James Barke: a Great Hearted Writer, a Hater of Oppression, a True Scot", in Andy Croft (ed) *A Weapon in the Struggle. The Cultural History of the Communist Party in Britain.* London & Sterling Virginia, Pluto Press, 1998, p. 24.

77. NLS MS27065 ff. 8–11. I am grateful to John Manson for giving me a copy of this document.

78. *Twentieth Century France. Politics and Society 1898–1991.* London, New York, Melbourne, Auckland, Edward Arnold, 1992, p. 111.

79. Degras (ed.) Vol. III, p. 384.

80. *Raucle Tongue, The II,* p. 538 italics in original.

81. See A. Rossi, *A Communist Party in Action. An Account of the Organization and Operations in France,* translated By Wilmoore Kendall, New Haven, Yale University Press, 1949.

82. Reprinted in *New Scotland* 30 November 1936.

83. *Ibid.,* p. 537.

84. *Ibid.,* p. 540.

85. *New Scotland* October 1935.

86. *New Scotland* 30 November 1936.

87. *Ibid.,* The quote was from the General Secretary of the Comintern, Georgi Dimitrov, who had become world famous for his defence at the Reichstag Fire trial in 1933.

88. *Ibid.*

89. "Scottish Culture and Imperialist War*", Raucle Tongue, The III*, pp. 7–8; original in Sir Norman Angell *et al.*, *Eleventh Hour Questions*, Edinburgh & London, The Moray Press, 1937, p. 109.

90. *Raucle Tongue, The III*, p. 6, Angell *et al*, p. 107.

91. "The Last War and the Present", Angell *et al*, pp. 80–84.

92. Degras Vol. III, pp. 372–3.
93. *Raucle Tongue, The II*, p. 536.
94. *New Scotland* 30th. November 1935.
95. Nina Fishman, *The British Communist Party and the Trade Unions 1933–45*, Aldershot, Scoular Press, 1995, p. 32.
96. *Raucle Tongue, The III*, p. 13.
97. Aitken Ferguson, *Scotland*, Glasgow, the Communist Party of Great Britain (Scottish District Committee), 1938, p. 28.
98. *Ibid.*
99. *Ibid.*, p. 29.
100. *Ibid.*, p. 30.
101. PH Scott & AC Davis (eds.), The Age of MacDiarmid, Edinburgh, 1980, p. 20.
102. See Noreen Branson, *History of the Communist Party of Great Britain, 1927–41*, London, Lawrence & Wishart, 1985, pp. 288–90.
103. Keith Laybourn & Dylan Murphy, *Under the Red Flag, A History of Communism in Britain c.1848–1991*, Stroud, Sutton Publishing, 1999. p. 111.
104. *New Selected Letters* p. 189.
105. John Manson, *Hugh MacDiarmid: the Poet and the Party.*

Red and Tartan

MacDiarmid Communist and Nationalist

> I fight in red for the same reasons
> That Garibaldi chose the red shirt
> Because a few men in a field wearing red
> Look like many men – if there are ten you will think
> There are a hundred; if a hundred
> You will believe them a thousand.
> And the colour red dances in the enemy's rifle sights
> And his aim will be bad – But best reason of all,
> A man in a red shirt can neither hide nor retreat.
>
> ("Why I Choose Red", from *Lucky Poet*.)[1]

MacDiarmid's political life changed direction during the Second World War. In 1941 he was mobilised into war production and his long Shetland exile ended, he moved with his family to Glasgow where he could once again be politically active. But the world he had known in the '20s and '30s was changing fundamentally, war was forging solidarity between the UK's component nations and in 1945, despite SNP successes in war-time by-elections, the Scots voted overwhelmingly for a Labour Government and a renewed United Kingdom.

The political stresses of war the split the SNP and this allowed him to be readmitted to membership, but friction with its new leaders was as great as it had been in the National Party of Scotland. During the Cold War he returned to the Communist Party where he remained for the rest of his life, but this did not prevent him from continuing to participate in fringe nationalist groups.

Imperialism against Nazism

Soon after war broke out, he and his friend Sorley MacLean discussed the issues it raised for Scotland. The Gaelic poet had joined the Signals Corps, despite his reservations about taking the side of the

British Empire. He believed that a Nazi victory would be disastrous, Scotland would become a puppet state like Slovakia and the survival of the USSR would be jeopardised.[2] MacDiarmid thought that the Nazis could not win. They were probably more "murderously destructive" in the short term, but the French and British bourgeoisie were able to win the war and in the long term they, were a "far greater enemy."[3] The two friends were on opposite sides of what is now seen as a fundamental cleavage within Western civilisation, but they regarded their disagreements as matters of emphasis and tactics, not of principle.

MacDiarmid was reading the anti-war propaganda of Arthur Donaldson's *Scottish News and Comment, The Scots Socialist,* newspaper of the Scottish Socialist Party,[4] and Palme Dutt's editorials in *Labour Monthly.*[5] In the early stages of the war Donaldson believed that Britain would be defeated and that Scotland would probably get a better deal from a German victory. The Scottish Socialist Party was a tiny group of propagandists founded in 1939 by J. Harrison Miller (Harry Miller) to "continue the John MacLean tradition" of agitation against conscription and imperialist war.[6] Palme Dutt, the leading ideologist of the CPGB, laid down the Comintern's anti-war line during the period of the pact between Nazi Germany and the USSR.

MacDiarmid was not alone in regarding the British ruling class as an equal, or greater, enemy than the Axis. His friend Archie Lamont, pleading before a Conscientious Objectors' Tribunal in 1942, was one of a vocal minority:

> The small man and the small state were being driven to the wall. On all sides one was told that State Socialism, which he presumed to be the same as ... State Capitalism and Bureaucratic Despotism was inevitable after the war. Apart from the monstrous persecution of the Jews, that seemed to be very much what Hitler himself was fighting for.[7]

Sentiments of this kind were not just a Scottish phenomenon, Stephen Howe quotes Fenner Brockway of the ILP arguing, in 1942, that Nazism and British Imperialism were both "Capitalist Dictatorships" which persecuted those whom they regarded as racially inferior,

> Is it not clear that that no Socialist – indeed no sincere democrat – can identify himself with Imperialism against Nazism, or can be satisfied with an end of the war which would destroy the Nazi dictatorship only?"[8]

Brockway and those who thought like him were holding on to ideas and principles that had stemmed from the struggle against conscription and militarism during the First World War. Such ideas can seem inexplicable in the light of the unprecedented evil of Nazism. But, before 1945, few could have foreseen the Holocaust, nor could they have predicted that victory over the Axis would shatter the British Empire.

An English Imperialist Manoeuvre

The war precipitated divisions within Scottish nationalism.[9] Almost all SNP members saw the Axis powers as a threat to small nations, particularly after the invasions of the Low Countries and Norway. The leadership pledged support for the war effort, but some members were outright pacifists and many were opposed to conscription of Scots men and women by a London government.[10]

A few saw the war as a product of English perfidy, in July 1939 the Scottish Neutrality League, led by Arthur Donaldson, declared:

> Any war into which England may enter, no matter the pretext, will be for the preservation of her World Empire, the suppression of dangerous trade rivals or to prevent the rise of a dominant nation on the continent of Europe. In none of these has Scotland any interest ...[11]

The leaders of the SNP were embarrassed by the activities of an anti-war group called "United Scotland". Its principal spokesperson was Arthur Donaldson and its Executive Council contained three veterans of the old London Branch of the NPS, Angus Clarke, Hugh Paterson and Iain Gillies – all now living in Scotland.[12] They still regarded Scottish sovereignty as the main issue, as Donaldson put it, "... Scotland must have a government whose powers shall be unlimited within its own borders and in its own affairs and which shall be answerable only to its own people."[13] But United Scotland was a disparate organisation and another leading member was Harry Miller, his Scottish Socialist Party took a similar view to Brockway's, and campaigned on issues of imperialism and civil liberties.

MacDiarmid supported United Scotland although, living on Whalsey, he could not be actively involved. In a letter to Thomas Johnston, Secretary of State for Scotland, of May 1941, he protested about the detention of Arthur Donaldson and police raids on the *Scots Socialist* and other nationalist opponents of the war. He described the operation as, "a base English Imperialist manoeuvre to throttle and libel the growing Scottish Socialist Republican Movement."[14] But only the Scottish Socialist Party could be described in this way. Donaldson, a former Chrysler executive in Detroit, was far from being a socialist.[15] Even Archie Lamont, despite the fact that he had done "much to stimulate the ideal of a Self-Governing Scotland amongst socialists ... remained simply a Scottish nationalist."[16]

What held United Scotland together was their belief that the centralising tendencies of the war-time British state gave Scotland little to choose between Nazi Germany and an imperialist London government[17] and they were united in their opposition to conscription. But although MacDiarmid agreed with them about the war, he could not have regarded conscription as a matter of principle because did not resist when he was conscripted into industry in 1941. In fact his letters to his wife Valda were positively enthusiastic about his new work.[18]

Quoting Ouspensky

In 1942 the anti-conscription poet Douglas Young was elected President of the SNP[19] defeating John MacCormick's favoured candidate William Power. MacCormick had lost control of the Party and he walked out, together with nearly half the membership. MacDiarmid's bitterest nationalist opponent had departed and the new leadership consisted of people he perceived as friends and allies, so it was possible for him to rejoin. After the split, as Jack Brand writes, "most of those who were left were 'true believers' who would fight to keep party doctrine pure."[20] Their doctrine was that of Arthur Donaldson, "complete independence and constitutional means to achieve independence ... ".[21] They were also striving to build "a serious party which would fight parliamentary elections."[22] MacDiarmid agreed with their insistence on independence, but not with their electoral strategy and he rejoined at time when, as in the 1930s, nationalist success was followed by frustration and failure.

In April 1945, Dr. Robert Macintyre won the Motherwell and Wishaw by-election with 51.4% and became the first ever Scottish Nationalist MP. In two earlier by-elections the Party had scored 37% and 41.3%. However, the following July, Macintyre lost the seat at the General Election. By the time of the 1945 election the SNP only had resources to field eight candidates and it scored an average of just over 8.5% in the seats it fought. In five by-elections between 1946 and 1948 it achieved an average of just over 9%. MacDiarmid fought

Glasgow Kelvingrove as an SNP candidate in 1945, getting 4.9%.[23] (He may not have increased his vote by quoting the esoteric Russian philosopher Ouspensky at his main election meeting).[24] In the face of these reversals the new leadership carried on doggedly, organising branches and fighting elections. MacDiarmid was intellectually and temperamentally unsuited for this style of politics and a clash was inevitable.

The Party Caucus

He had become a member of the SNP's National Council at Douglas Young's invitation, but his relationship with his colleagues were almost as difficult as it had been ten years earlier. When his 1945 candidacy in Kelvingrove was discussed, Austin Walker, the Vice-Chairman, moved that the Party withdraw its endorsement because MacDiarmid had declared that he was not a democrat and believed in the dictatorship of the proletariat. Robert Macintyre seconded, asking MacDiarmid about his alleged anti-English election speech in Kelvingrove. However William Aitken argued that it was not advisable to withdraw endorsement from a candidate at this late stage and, by sixteen votes to four the Council upheld MacDiarmid's nomination.[25]

The breaking point came over a seemingly trivial issue. In July 1945, there was a proposal to set up a committee to appoint a new caretaker for the SNP premises. MacDiarmid remarked that it would be "advisable to have someone outside the Party 'caucus.'" Dr. Macintyre took exception, and MacDiarmid was asked to withdraw his remarks. He replied that, "he would make the position easier by resigning from the Council and the Party." This averted a clash with Donaldson, who intended to confront MacDiarmid over an allegation about election funding. Archie Lamont moved that MacDiarmid be asked to return, but was defeated by thirteen votes to eight.[26]

This was not his final breach with the SNP, but he was now on the periphery of the Party and becoming increasingly disillusioned. In 1947 he fulminated against the leadership for expelling supporters of Robert Blair Wilkie and the Scottish Resistance Committee,

> Practically every well known Nationalist of any intellectual ability has been excluded by the little group of 'Tooley Street Tailors' who run this odd organisation. Unredeemed mediocrity is the only passport to secure membership. In these circumstances the SNP is doing more harm than good and is, in fact, preventing the growth of the Nationalist movement.[27]

His second involvement with nationalist politics was bound to fail because he had too little in common with the other Scottish nationalists. He rejected the SNP's turn to electoral politics and opposed McCormick's attempts to create a cross-party consensus. He was not interested in Arthur Donaldson's theory of sovereignty and he also differed from Douglas Young, who was radical only on the issue of conscription. He appeared to have most in common with the Scottish Socialist Party, like him they lauded John MacLean and propounded a left wing version of Scottish nationalism. But their socialism was eclectic and sentimental, in the ILP tradition which he had left behind quarter of a century earlier.

The Disingenuous Plea

The Scottish nationalist movement remained fragmented until the early 1970s. The SNP continued to be led by Arthur Donaldson and Robert Macintyre, who stuck to their electoral strategy despite many disappointments. MacCormick's Scottish Convention became the largest grouping, but there was a was a great deal of overlap in the membership of the various groups. At the beginning of February 1950 *The National Weekly,* an independent nationalist journal, convened a conference of the "splinter parties" who intended to put up candidates in the forthcoming general election. The conference unanimously agreed that MacDiarmid should stand in Kelvingrove. He initially said that he would run as an independent, but he was persuaded to adopt the label "Independent Scottish Nationalist."[28] Most of his election workers came from the Scottish Resistance Committee.

In the event, nine nationalist candidates (only three from the SNP) stood under six different labels. They spanned a spectrum from Major Hume Sleigh on the extreme right to MacDiarmid on the pro-Communist left. Every single deposit was lost and the average vote fell from the 8.5% of 1945 to 3.75% – MacDiarmid achieved only 2.09%. No nationalist group was strong enough to draw the different strands together, so that the fragmentation persisted.

The most active group became MacCormick's Convention, its Scottish Covenant was signed by nearly two million Scots, an impressive achievement which showed that voting patterns at elections did not reflect the Scottish public's attitudes to the Union.[29] MacDiarmid was critical of the Covenant because it petitioned Westminster for a limited measure of Home Rule and expressed loyalty to the Crown, nevertheless, in his Kelvingrove election address he appealed for votes from its signatories.[30]

I hope the Covenant will be signed by a very high percentage of our people. It is the best thing they can do.... The reasons I gave for refusing to sign ... depended largely on the wording ... and the entirely disingenuous plea of the promoters that it transcended all party politics. Instead of that its framers, by chicane, dragged in all their personal 'political' prejudices and predictions.[31]

If their intentions had sincere, he claimed, they would have sought out what all nationalists had in common. In other words, they should have produced a document based on the aspirations of the nationalist fragments, not what might appeal to most Scots. When the supporters of the Covenant convened a "Scottish National Assembly" in Edinburgh 1948 MacDiarmid castigated it and returned to one of his most persistent themes. It "... showed no concern for anything more than the satisfaction of certain petty contemporary appetites. It was not illuminated by any master idea."[32] After the election he blamed the disastrous result on MacCormick and the other leaders of Scottish Convention, who had not given a strong lead to the signatories of the Covenant. He went further, "the very name 'Scottish Nationalist' is now hopelessly prejudiced", and he believed that he would have done better in Kelvingrove if he had stood simply as an independent.[33]

In his 1945 campaign he had directed his fire against his Conservative opponent, the former Secretary of State Walter Elliot, whom he denounced as an "English Quisling."[34] But in 1950 he flagged up foreign policy issues of current interest to the Communist Party. He attacked "... the so-called Labour Government", which

... was imposing military conscription in peacetime and incurring the heaviest armaments bill in British history. They would find it incredible that a British Labour Government should have spent hundreds of millions of pounds backing up a Fascist monarchical regime in Greece and suppressing national independence movements in Malaya and elsewhere....[35]

In the background was the unfolding Cold War. From the promulgation of the Truman Doctrine in March 1947, to the founding of NATO in April 1949, the former wartime allies had been dividing into two hostile camps. The division was not only geographical, it ran through their societies, with minorities in North America and Europe standing by the Soviet Union and the Warsaw Pact states. In 1950 this international trend was reflected in Scotland, the former Communist MP Willie Gallacher lost his West Fife seat, his vote slumping by nearly half compared with 1945. As the Cold War plunged to icy new depths and public opinion became increasingly hostile towards the USSR and domestic Communists, MacDiarmid's priorities shifted. This was one reason for his involvement in the Scotland USSR Friendship Society, through which he began his trek back to the CPGB.

Totalitarianism in Scotland

Neal Wood categorised MacDiarmid as one of those former Communists who, "remain silent about their differences with the Party and continue to support its general policy."[36] This is misleading because, as late as August 1945 he was still alienated from the CPGB, describing his former comrades as "analphabetic street orators."[37] But even if he had preferred stay with the SNP, this became impossible as Cold War ideology exerted its influence.

In May 1946 Alex Murray, writing in the *Scots Independent*, denounced the British and the Soviet governments. They were imperialist, despite the fact that "... both profess to be 'socialist'". The annexation of the Baltic states and the occupation of Poland in 1939 had shown the true character of the "Bolshevik World Drive." Communist subversion could be seen in China, Belgium, France, Greece, Yugoslavia and Canada. It was true that English agents had also been stirring up trouble, but "the Stalinists are worse." If this led to war, "Scots should join the anti-Bolshevik, anti-Imperialist alliance, but ONLY WHEN SCOTLAND IS HERSELF FREE FROM ENGLISH CONTROL."

MacDiarmid responded vigorously, asking "Why Should Scots Fight Russians?" He blamed the influence of "London controlled newspapers" for the growing anti-Soviet feeling in Scotland and within the Labour movement. This sentiment would not last long, the Labour Government's "programme of nationalisation simply means a vast extension of London control." The Scots would wish, "... that they lived under a system which, as in Soviet Russia conceded a large measure of autonomy to its component parts and not under a system of English ascendancy",[38] he also drummed the WW2 beat of opposition to conscription. But his claim that the USSR guaranteed minority national rights made little impression on Scottish nationalists as they saw, one by one, the East European states being incorporated into the Soviet Bloc, culminating in the Communist coup in Czechoslovakia of February 1948.

In April 1949, using a newly popular term, the *Scots Independent* declared that the SNP would have nothing to do with "Totalitarianism in any shape or form, Communist or Fascist." It denounced the tactics of infiltration and subversion that had been used by the Communists in Eastern Europe, most recently in Czechoslovakia. It quoted the poet

Maurice Lindsay, who had attacked attempts to, "turn the Scottish Renaissance into a Communist racket", and it went on,

> ... certain of its leaders, while concerned at bottom with Scottish literature, are being innocently used by Communists in Scotland for their own ends. And the tragedy is that the people being used would probably be the first to be liquidated if Communism were ever to come to force in Scotland.

This was a direct message to MacDiarmid – Communists were not going be tolerated within the SNP.

And less open influences were at work. An unsigned article in the *Scots Independent* of July 1950 reported a conference held in Edinburgh the previous month. It had been organised by the Scottish League for European Freedom and had gathered together "representatives of many nations at present under Russian domination."[39] The League was mainly a voice for exiles from the Ukraine and, it has been alleged, was funded by MI6.[40] In 1953 the Chairman of the League, John F. Stewart and George McAlister of the Scotland USSR Society debated Scottish trade with the Soviet Union in the *Scottish Journal*, a nationalist publication. McAlister made the tactical mistake of using "Russia" as a generic term for the USSR while Stewart portrayed it as a "prison of nations." His claims about the brutal treatment of the small Baltic states would have been particularly influential with SNP members.[41]

A Genuine Social Democracy

Even without such external influences, the idea of national liberation from Russian tyranny would have appealed to Scottish nationalists. The idea had first been trailed in January 1940, when the *Scots Independent* labelled the Soviet invasion of Finland "Czarist Communism". After the Nazi the invasion of its territory, the contribution of the Soviet Union to the struggle against the Axis was praised, but the Cold War changed perceptions once more. Responding to the outbreak of the Korean war, Robert Macintyre sought to recast the SNP's philosophy,

> Russian Communism can make no inroads into a stable and just society where personal responsibility is widely diffused, where the level of education is high, and where class differences are not deep. Such countries are the self-governing Scandinavian nations which have a genuine social democracy. So would a self-governing Scotland.[42]

Two months later he criticised the Labour Government for its policy towards Europe and its autarchic, state socialist, economic policy. He called for,

1. A Scottish Government and Parliament responsible to the Scottish people;
2. an end to isolation from Europe and a voice in a European Assembly;
3. the ownership of Scotland by her people in such a way that an overwhelming proportion of her people directly own the country.[43]

This was a "third way", similar to European Christian Democracy. It opposed the unrestrained culture of free enterprise in the United States, the centralised state socialism practised by the USSR and the democratic variant that was being implemented by the 1945 Labour Government. The SNP and MacDiarmid had moved further apart and there was no prospect of a reconciliation.

Communist Dominated Movements

MacDiarmid drew closer to the Communist Party after collaborating with them in a rally to commemorate the 25th anniversary of the death of John Maclean, which occurred in January 1948. This was held under the auspices of the Scotland-USSR Society and it marked the fact that the Bolshevik government of 1917 had appointed MacLean as the first Soviet Consul in Scotland.

In March 1949 MacDiarmid wrote that he was, "very active in the Scottish-USSR Society and am more and more being involved in all manner of associated near Communist, Peace, and Anti-Fascist bodies …"[44] By March 1950 he was, "… a Communist – not a member, just now, of the CP, but hand in glove with and working for all the 'Communist dominated' movements in this country…."[45] In February 1952 he was quite open about his position.

> I have not rejoined, because it is felt that at this juncture I am much more useful to the CP as I am than as I would be as a member. I speak for them, the *Daily Worker* gives me a good press. I generally take the chair for Russian and Chinese delegations visiting Scotland, and so on, I am a Vice President of the British Peace Committee, President of the Scottish Youth and Students Union, and a director of Theatre Workshop Ltd. A purely Communist body….[46]

It was not unusual for Party supporters, who were also public figures, to remain what Neal Wood called "crypto-members."[47] They could promote the Party's various front organisations and were particularly useful in lending their names to peace campaigns, which sought to rouse public opinion in the West against NATO's military build-up in Western Europe.

When MacDiarmid wrote to John Gollan, the General Secretary of the CPGB, on 15th November 1956, suggesting that he should resume his membership, he was actually proposing that he should come out openly as the Communist he had been for years. He now claimed that the Party had made significant concessions on Scottish issues. But, while it no longer denied the significance of the national identity of the Scots, and it had accepted the need for specific polices to suit Scottish circumstances, it never endorsed any more radical form of self-government than a devolved parliament within the UK.[48]

He rejoined a chastened Party. After the twin blows of Khrushchev's revelations about Stalin and the invasion of Hungary it had suffered a serious loss of members, particularly amongst intellectuals. Rigid conformity could no longer be imposed and, now that he was recognised as a great Scottish poet, MacDiarmid's deviations from Communist orthodoxy, (which were still significant) were not subjected to scrutiny. He continued in membership for the rest of his life, but this was largely symbolic. He was not active in a branch and did not get involved in the Party's internal discussions, his most public contribution to the Party was in the general election of 1964, when he stood as the Communist candidate in Kinross and West Perthshire, against the Prime Minister Sir Alec Douglas Home. This was a challenge to the restrictions on political broadcasting by minor parties and his campaign was vindicated when the legislation was amended to allow such broadcasts, in proportion to party votes.

He now used his position as Scotland's most celebrated living poet to speak in defence of the Soviet Union, its allies, and its international policies. In June 1945 he made a speech at the Scottish Congress for Friendship and Co-operation with the USSR in which he, "outlined the literary associations between Scotland and Russia and praised the interest shown today by the Russians in Scottish Poetry and the Arts."[49] The Congress had its origins in the grass roots "Aid to Russia" committees that had sprung up during the War and its sponsors included three Lord Provosts, nine "Reverends" and a number of noted writers, artists and academics. It proceeded to set up the Scotland-USSR Society and MacDiarmid was elected to the Executive Committee. The Society stated that it did not seek to, "champion any political or social system",[50] but a visitor to one of its concerts observed a huge hammer and sickle flag dominating the stage, together with portraits of Lenin, Stalin and Marx.[51] In 1946 the Labour Party declared it to be, "an organisation ancillary and subservient to the Communist Party."[52]

The Counter-revolutionary Danger

The most controversial aspect of MacDiarmid's politics in these years was his support for the suppression of the Hungarian Revolution in 1956. In a letter to the *Daily Worker* of March 1957 he announced that he was rejoining the Communist Party, "... to rally to the Party again and throw all my energies into the fight."[53] He wanted to resume his membership because his principal concern had now become the threat to the USSR. He was "convinced of the counter-revolutionary danger" in Hungary, which was being "fomented by American and other capitalist powers and by the Roman Catholic Church". He believed that the invasion was "not only justified but imperative, if unfortunately necessary."

This is given added drama when contrasted with the resignations from the CPGB of many other intellectuals at that time. But, like most historical dramas, it omits a good deal of complexity. Shortly before he wrote to Gollan, MacDiarmid had signed an open letter, together with fourteen other Communist intellectuals, which criticised the CPGB leadership. It was printed in *Tribune* and the *New Statesman* on 18th November and had originally been submitted to the *Daily Worker,* but rejected by the editor. The letter denounced the leadership's responses to Khrushchev's revelations about Stalin and the invasion of Hungary. It called on the them to repudiate their errors of judgement and to realise that Marxist ideas would only "be acceptable to the to the British labour movement if they arise from the truth about the world we live in."[54]

In his biography of MacDiarmid, Alan Bold suggested that this "open letter" and the one announcing his resumption of membership, contradicted each other,[55] but the truth is more complex. MacDiarmid sympathised with aspects of the case being made by the dissidents and he sent his friend, the Communist artist Barbara Niven, a copy of *The Reasoner.* This bulletin was issued by Edward Thompson and John Saville of the Yorkshire District of the CP for distribution only to Party members. They were distressed by the silence of the leadership of the CPGB about what they had known of Stalin's terror. The editors stressed,

> *The Reasoner* was conceived entirely in terms of the general interests of the Party. It is not, and we do not intend to allow it to become, a journal of faction.... recent events have made it plain that without the right of free, open and unfettered discussion Communist parties will become victims of the disease of orthodoxy ... we believed that the widespread discontent – vague, un-formulated, often very emotional – would harden in bitterness, frustration or anti-Party attitudes....[56]

MacDiarmid did not see their actions as hostile to the Party, and he told his friend,

> I was very sorry to hear it had been suppressed – just why I could not make out. While in some ways perhaps not too bad for a start the *Reasoner* didn't go very far and I am convinced it is quite essential to go into matters a great deal more thoroughly and without any respect of persons and without any hedging in inter-party (let alone any other) criticism.[57]

He may have remembered the charge against him, twenty years earlier, of publishing *The Voice of Scotland* without permission. Thompson and Saville were being treated in the same unimaginative and bureaucratic manner and it was logical to sympathise with them on this particular point.

So there are, in fact, *four* letters that have to be reconciled. The one to Barbara Niven and the "open letter" both supported greater tolerance of discussion within the CPBG. The ones to John Gollan and the *Daily Worker* expressed solidarity with the Party and the USSR. They seem incompatible only if it is assumed that the sole issue was the invasion, and if the events of 1956 are viewed backwards, through their eventual, tragic, outcome.

The "open letter" was dated 4th November 1956, Imre Nagy and the other leaders of the overthrown Hungarian government were not executed until June 1958, so that the full impact of what was happening was still unfolding when MacDiarmid agreed to sign. The November 1956 issue of *The Reasoner* (its third and final edition) carried Edward Thompson's "Through the Smoke of Budapest" and this became the catalyst for mass resignations from the CPGB, not only of intellectuals but of trade unionists and many rank and file members. Until this point the issues of internal party democracy and the invasion could be regarded as separate matters. That is probably why the joint letter had an addendum, "Not all the signatories agree with everything in this letter, but all are in sufficient sympathy with its general intentions to sign with this reservation."[58] This would have allowed MacDiarmid to sign in good conscience. His support for the protest against the Party leadership, while also backing the Soviet invasion, may have been unusual, but it was not incoherent.

When the mass resignations led to the creation of the "New Left", he cleaved more closely to the Party, denouncing these ex-members as "... sucklings of that mother they are now seeking to devour ..."[59] In an unpublished letter sent to *Encounter* in March 1957 he took issue with remarks made by the Scottish American poet Burns Singer.

"Although, ... I signed the *New Statesman* letter, I never had any intention of throwing out the Marxist baby with the humanitarian bath-water. But I would not have signed it if I had been a member of the C.P."[60] In other words, his signature had been prompted by the leadership's handling of internal debate, but once the crisis had split the Party, and world Communism had come under unprecedented attack, he rallied to its side.

A Golden Age

In 1950 MacDiarmid visited the Soviet Union, as part of a delegation organised by the Scotland-USSR Society. He returned declaring that, "... the USSR is the greatest leap forward in the history of humanity." Scottish workers would be amazed at the "shops crammed with food" at "prices within the reach of every housewife's purse". The people were "well clad" and "the housing problem has been solved...."[61] Purchasing power had been "repeatedly increased in the last four or five years and the proportion of national income spent on the armed forces ... repeatedly cut ..."[62] He wrote enthusiastically to his son Michael about the sumptuous food he had enjoyed, after the austerity of post-war Scotland such hospitality was bound to have impressed him.[63]

He would not have known about the food riots in Kharkov in the winter of 1946–7,[64] and he seems not to have reflected that, five years after the greatest war in human history, a decrease in Soviet military expenditure was to be expected. In reality 1949 was the year of the Soviet atom bomb and one economist found evidence that military and heavy industrial expenditure were given such a priority that, "... its industry turned out less than one pair of shoes per Soviet citizen. And in the war-devastated western areas ... millions still lived in caves, dugouts, rickety huts, and other makeshift habitations because conventional housing was lacking."[65]

The Scottish visitors would have been steered well away from such sights, it was established practice to treat guests of the USSR lavishly, while shielding them from the real conditions being endured by the people. But, according to Ronald Grigor Suny, MacDiarmid's account of conditions was not completely inaccurate.

Each year from 1948 to 1954 the government lowered prices on many essential goods such as bread, which by the mid-1950s cost half what it cost in 1947. Decades later many older people would remember the late Stalin period as a golden age of peace, low prices, and strict, predictable, order.[66]

There is a similar complexity in his report of his visit to the Republic of Georgia. He praised the way in which the nationalities policy of the USSR was being applied, but he did not mention the republic's history of nationalist dissent and the political persecution that followed its forcible incorporation into the Soviet Union in the 1920s. Six years after MacDiarmid's visit hundreds of demonstrators were killed when Red Army troops opened fire. Ironically, they were protesting about Khrushchev's denunciation of their local hero Joseph Stalin, but the incident shows how uneasy Georgia's position actually was. Nevertheless he was not entirely deluded when he praised its cultural achievements. Robert Parsons of the BBC Russian World Service confirmed that, in this period, "Soviet policies seem to have strengthened Georgian national identity." And, on Parsons' evidence, MacDiarmid was not mistaken when he described increased living standards and significant medical advances in Georgia at that time.[67]

Cuckoo-Cloudland

He had enlisted on the side of the USSR and he supported it in the cultural joustings that were a feature of the times. All over the world, two social and political systems were competing for support from artists and intellectuals, so that the Cold War, "... was simultaneously a traditional politico-military confrontation between two empires ... and at the same time an ideological and cultural contest on a global scale and without historical precedent."[68] MacDiarmid was called on to tour the Soviet bloc, giving readings and lectures and take part in cultural events and peace conferences. He visited, China, Bulgaria, East Germany, Hungary, Poland, the USSR and Yugoslavia (before the breach between Tito and Stalin). When he returned he give glowing accounts of what he had seen and he rejected the claims of defectors about the repression of critics and the brutal treatment of large sections of the population. He resolutely refused to believe in the existence of the Gulag and its Siberian labour camps, describing their alleged location as "Cuckoo-Cloudland."[69]

Angus Calder commented that MacDiarmid,

> ... remained his own man when travelling abroad with his party card. He continued to praise Joyce and Ezra Pound loudly when Western Modernism was still anathema to Eastern Marxist orthodoxy, he continued to extol the executed Pasternak, and in due contrast he paid due tribute surprisingly rarely to the indubitably great Communist poets of the century Brecht and Neruda.[70]

But in an interview of 1975, in which he praised Pasternak and Heine, MacDiarmid described Aleksandr Solzhenitsyn as "a malignant enemy of the Soviet system", he was "simply a sensational reporter" who would have been subject to a imprisonment if he had been a Western writer making similar attacks on his own country.[71] In this, as in much of what he had to say about USSR, there was a stubborn refusal to consider that he might be mistaken.

An example of his credulity was the Lysenko affair. From 1930 to 1965 the Soviet state promoted the genetic theories of the agronomist Trofim Lysenko and persecuted his critics. Lysenko, who contradicted the prevailing genetic theories of Gregor Mendel, claimed that the environment in which plants are grown could produce changes that would be passed on to succeeding generations. Experts outside the USSR maintained that Mendel was right, and that there was no evidence that stable, inherited, genetic changes could be induced by external conditions.

Eventually Lysenko was discredited, after significant damage had been done to Soviet agriculture. But in 1949 MacDiarmid, who had no expertise in genetic science defended him.[72] He cited the work of Luther Burbank, an American plant breeder of the early twentieth century, who had become famous for breeding a new and hardier potato. (Burbank's was mother was born in Scotland and MacDiarmid claimed him as a "Scottish genius"). But when Burbank's methods were scrutinised on behalf of the Carnegie Institution it was found that they, ". . . cannot give any confirmation of Mendelism or any other theory of inheritance that rests upon statistical inquiry."[73] Burbank was not Scottish, he was not a scientist and his work had not disproved Mendel's laws of genetics.

And he ignored at least one case of cruel injustice about which he should have known. Prince D. S. Mirsky, a White Russian émigré, had become an admirer of the USSR under Stalin, for patriotic reasons. He joined the British Communist Party and returned to Russia where he was arrested and died in the Gulag.[74] MacDiarmid had dedicated his *First Hymn to Lenin* to Mirsky, but he seems to have made no attempt to find out what happened to him.

An Anti-Utopian Utopia

MacDiarmid believed that the USSR was an advance in the history of human civilisation but, unlike most other Western Communists, he did not share in the cult of Stalin. Some of his poetry did present Lenin and Stalin, symbolically, as "philosopher rulers" but his political writings made very little reference to either of them. He was not completely uncritical, just as he had not endorsed the Moscow Trials in the 1930s, he did not join in the clamour against Tito and Yugoslavia in 1948, nor did he support the trial and execution of the Czechoslovak leader Rudolf Slánský in 1959. At the founding of the Scottish Congress for Friendship and Co-operation with the USSR he said that there had to be,

> *... freedom in transplanting the lessons we learn from the U.S.S.R.*
> *to Scottish soil, interpreting them according to our own traditions*
> *and needs,* and applying them to the solution of our own problems,
> and thus associating ourselves with the development of Soviet
> Russia's influence in the world in the most intimate and effective
> way, the only way in which our friendship could be properly devel-
> oped and the future of mankind secured. [75]

MacDiarmid was a professional journalist, and in much of what he wrote about the USSR and the Bloc states he selected the evidence that would present these societies in a favourable light. But he gave occasional hints of internal misgivings, even when projecting unshakable certainty. In 1950 he wrote to Maurice Lindsay, "I regard the 'democratic' system in non-Communist countries as a monstrous fraud. Communism in my view is the only guarantee of individuality in the modern world and the USSR the only real democracy the world has yet seen."[76]

He believed that the danger to the arts in Britain and America did not come from the small minority of Communists but from those who were persecuting them and imposing artistic values that were "safe" for the existing order.[77]

> I want you to understand that I have chosen my side and am
> utterly and irrevocably opposed to Christianity, capitalism, and
> all the social *and artistic forms* these have produced or that are
> compatible with them. This must lead to a state of civil war –
> indeed people of my point of view are already all but outlawed in
> this country and the United States.[78]

But an earlier letter to Lindsay contained a partial admission.

> The fusion of political propaganda and literary criticism is by
> no means peculiar to the Soviet Union, and is not necessarily
> dishonest in any case. If we Communists make our political bias
> more obtrusive, that is more honest – the fact is that reactionaries
> are none the less pushing their propaganda just as persistently,
> if more insidiously, all the time.... I do not agree with you
> that there is less freedom of the artist in the Soviet Union than
> in Britain or the United States, only the incidence of lets and
> hindrances is different.[79]

He went on to cite compulsory education in Britain and the USSR as equal in their acculturation of children into their respective systems. But, although he did not accept that there was repression in the USSR, he suggested that a Communist state in the British Isles would utilise methods more in tune with their political traditions.

He elaborated his argument about "freedom" a couple of years later in a letter to the poet and editor Peter Russell:

> ... like many anti-Communists you seem to me to argue from *a priori* grounds. The use of the term "free world" is a case in point. So is the usual religious argument – viz. that unless a God is predicated, the world can't make sense. My reply is that I find more freedom in the USSR – the 'freedom' of the Western Democracies is mostly misused; the right to be ignorant, the right of stupid people to express what they call opinions when they lack the means of forming any, the right to publish rubbish even when the effect is to sabotage that compulsory 'education' on which so much money is spent etc.[80]

He was drawing attention to one kind of freedom, the right of a society not to be permeated by trashy culture, and suggesting that it could be traded against the freedom to publish and discuss ideas that are critical of the state. And he was trying to prove the superiority of the Soviet system by referring to shortcomings in capitalist civilisation. This kind of slanted polemic was all too common on both sides during the Cold War. But MacDiarmid's arguments also carried an echo of his Apollinian/Faustian dichotomy in *Albyn*. The West was "Apollinian" – brash and superficial, but the East was "Faustian", it had inner depths that were obscure to Western minds, dominated as they were by North American consumer culture.

The Farce of State Trials

In later years MacDiarmid's defence of the USSR became more cautious. In 1959 he tempered his usual praise for the rights of national minorities under the Stalin Constitution and admitted that "the extent to which that is exercised in actual practice is a debateable matter, perhaps...."[81] And, although he supported the invasion of Czechoslovakia in 1968 (despite the fact that the CPGB opposed it), he quoted approvingly from Dubček's final speech.[82]

He made a few apparently unconscious admissions, such as in praising the fact that a Soviet audience had known Pasternak's poems by heart even though, "they had not even been published – they had been circulated in roneo'd copies," (in other words in illegal Samizdat).[83] And he quoted the American critic Francis George Steiner,

> Even under Stalin, the writer and literary work played an vital role in Communist strategy. Writers were persecuted precisely because literature was recognised as an important and potentially dangerous force. This is a crucial point. Literature was being honoured in however cruel or perverted a way.[84]

This hints that, although he never commented on Khrushchev's 1956 speech denouncing Stalin, he accepted the truth of its revelations. And in a letter to his friend Major F.A.C. Boothby he wrote, "The farce of State Trials is not confined to the USSR."[85] In 1978 he was sufficiently suspicious to get a Russian translation of his *Third Hymn to Lenin* checked in Glasgow University, (he was told that the essence of the poem had been conveyed, but there were some modifications to make it conform more closely to the Party line).[86]

He remained convinced that, if there was justification for criticising the USSR, this should be weighed against the colonial atrocities of the British Empire and the racism and McCarthyism of the United States. For him the balance was overwhelmingly in favour of the Soviet Bloc, and he never resiled from this belief. However, the imperative to defend the USSR became less important in the late 1950s and the 1960s, as a new balance between East and West made a disastrous confrontation seem less likely. In these circumstances MacDiarmid became interested, once again, in Scotland and the nationalist movement.

Reactionaries, Poujadists and Philistines

The Communist Party tolerated his political idiosyncrasies and raised no objection to his continued involvement in fringe nationalist politics. The Scottish National Party had struggled on during the 1950s as "a modest family business"[87] fighting elections with meagre success, but new opportunities opened up in the early 1960s, created by the decline of the two party system. In 1967, the Party's fortunes were transformed when Winnie Ewing was elected MP for Hamilton. It rapidly became a mainstream Scottish party and the strategy developed by Arthur Donaldson and Robert Macintyre, of patient work in building branches and fighting elections, had finally succeeded. Then, after the discovery of oil in the North Sea, the SNP won support from the many Scots who now believed that Scotland could have a prosperous future outside the

Union. But MacDiarmid had always opposed populist politics of this kind and he was not willing to change his judgement merely because of electoral success.

> I have never been able to see that any good could come from the establishment in Edinburgh of a miniature replica of Westminster, with the same conception of politics, subscribing to the same economic system, and filled with M.P.s ignorant of and indifferent to our past achievements and present potentialities in a literature and other arts utterly from their English counterparts and making a contribution to world culture that only Scotland could make, and could make only in her own languages, Scots and Gaelic.[88]

In the late 1960s, a number of nationalist splinter groups still existed on the fringes of the SNP.[89] One of these was the 1320 Club, founded in 1967 with MacDiarmid as President. He described its purpose as, "to conduct research into various aspects of Scottish economy, culture, etc. with a view to having these thoroughly studied and the results available when, and if, Scottish independence is secured." According to MacDiarmid the 1320 Club was going to give the SNP, "effective intellectual backing" and it was "better equipped intellectually" than the SNP, who were "mere morons."[90]

The Club published a glossy magazine *Catalyst,* which carried some high quality political and literary contributions, many from independent writers. In October 1968 it organised a symposium on "Legal and Constitutional Aspects of Independence." One session was chaired by the writer, broadcaster, and human rights campaigner Ludovic Kennedy and two of the speakers were Professors of Law in Edinburgh University.[91] They produced some interesting observations on the legal status of the Treaty of Union, but the Club did not follow up these arguments. In fact its promises of innovative research and new thinking never materialised.

Another of its publications was a study of the defence needs of an independent Scotland, and this showed some of the problems the Club was creating for the SNP. It was a premature, to say the least, to raise the issue when the Party was still trying to consolidate its vote on the basis of its social and economic policies. And the pamphlet reverted to the old nationalist habit of spinning romantic fantasies. It advocated regular forces based on the historic Scottish regiments and, in addition, a voluntary, "territorial army thirled to its locality and wearing the tartan of that locality and the bonnet badge of the Regular Formation of the area."[92]

Any Policeman at the Bar

It was written by one of the most controversial figures in the national movement of the time, Major FAC (Derek) Boothby who was jailed briefly in 1975 as a consequence of his involvement in a shadowy "Army of the Provisional Government." It has also been alleged that he was a police agent and *agent provocateur*.[93] But Randall Foggie, who knew him in Edinburgh in the early 1960s, downplayed his importance,

> ... you'd meet him in Rose Street and he would say "have a dram" then "you know that pillar box on such and such with 'EIIR' on it? I think we ought to blow it up" – standing at the bar where everyone can hear. He would be too drunk by the time we decided to do it. He would talk about setting up a liberation army in the hills above Biggar, what would be need in the way of equipment etc. – any policeman at the bar would find it difficult to know whether anything real was meant. If he hadn't been so taken with drink and had actually done something about it the place would have been littered with dead bodies.[94]

John Herdman was appointed editor of *Catalyst* and discovered that Boothby expected him to take "advice" from Ronald MacDonald Douglas, an "elderly former journalist, short story writer and, in his own estimation, doughty freedom fighter."[95] When Herdman declined to accept the advice, he was ousted as editor and replaced by Douglas, who turned *Catalyst* into a cheaply produced vehicle for his own obsessions (it had run up huge debts by this time). One of these obsessions was Boothby, whom he now denounced as a police agent. The Major produced his own newsletter, entitled *Sgian Dubh*[96] and the two of them sniped at each other from their smudged and cramped pages.

The SNP National Council declared the 1320 Club incompatible with membership of the Party.[97] They were concerned about the fact that the Club's membership was secret and Winnie Ewing felt that its activities made her "vulnerable" to bad publicity in the press.[98] James Halliday recounts its attempts to get its supporters appointed as SNP branch officers (sometimes in a number of different branches simultaneously) in an attempt to "bring the entire party under their control."[99]

Boothby's fantasies about tartan-clad guerrillas and the rumours swirling around the pubs of Rose Street about secret armies, however ephemeral they may have been, were embarrassing for a Party that was firmly committed to constitutional methods. MacDiarmid, however, supported the Club's preparations for armed resistance.

> As with other struggles against Imperialism I do not believe that the Westminster Parliament will grant Scotland any useful measure of Self-Government no matter how strong the popular demand may be. Consequently contingency planning must include measures in case armed struggle is forced upon us.[100]

This was a long standing belief. More than thirty years earlier, in *Red Scotland,* he had declared that,

> England would resist not only Scottish independence but any real measure of devolution for Scotland far more viciously than it resisted Ireland's claim ... Militant methods would be necessary; there would have to be war between the two countries and probably civil war in Scotland itself.[101]

The 1320 Club, with its "broad" array of sponsors and its inner core of manipulative leaders was very like the front organisations in which MacDiarmid had worked on behalf of the Communist Party, except that neither Boothby nor Douglas were at all left wing and the 1320 Club's draft *Bill for the Government of Scotland* included a provision for the continuation of the monarchy.[102] What was MacDiarmid doing in such company? Part of the explanation is that he did not think in terms of traditional left/right dichotomies. As he wrote to Ronald MacDonald Douglas,

> You will know that for many years I have made a principle in my agitation for a psychological and political revolution in Scotland of what is called the 'Scottish Antisyzygy' i.e. the refusal to be channelled into a single course and the belief that contrariety rather then consensus is a good thing."[103]

Another reason was that he would have had very few personal friends if he had insisted on political agreement. On Randall Foggie's evidence, the Major was an engaging character[104] and MacDiarmid liked Boothby, who lived near him. He was even willing to excuse him if it turned out that he really was a police spy.[105] He wrote praising *Sgian Dubh* on two occasions, but he gave no specific examples of the courageous journalism he attributed to Boothby. It seems that his friend had asked him to write these pieces as a favour and he could not refuse.[106] He also approved of Douglas's takeover of *Catalyst,* and hoped it would become "… a genuinely revolutionary magazine and seek to regain the lost dynamic of the Scottish movement."[107] These were examples of his old habit of writing as if his own predictions were established facts, as he had done with Scottish Social Credit and *Clann Albainn.*

A Self-elected Elect

The 1320 Club provoked a broadside from MacDiarmid's old friend Hamish Henderson. The two had clashed four years earlier, about the Scottish folk song revival. Henderson was a pioneer collector of songs, and a promoter of traditional singers, in particular Jeannie Robertson from an Aberdeenshire Traveller family. She, "was recognised by a host of major academic figures. Just as important, she inspired a generation of revivalist singers who were searching for an exemplar with solid traditional roots."[108] Since Bulloch's praise of the Doric diminutive MacDiarmid had not favoured the Aberdeenshire tradition, and he was contemptuous:

> The demand everywhere today is for higher and higher intellectual levels. Why should we be concerned with songs which reflect the educational limitations, the narrow lives, the poor literary abilities, of a peasantry we have happily outgrown?[109]

The argument spilled over into their disagreement about the 1320 Club. Henderson attacked, "groups of self-elected Elect",

> … Gathered in disputatious huddles on the periphery of whatever rational and coherent activity they can find to disrupt, the self-elected Elect have done much to make Scottish self-government a subject for mockery not only south of the Border but among the broad masses of the Scottish people as well.[110]

MacDiarmid replied,

> His conception of 'democracy' is what concurs with majority opinion. Minorities are consequently to be vilified, and stigmatised as 'trouble makers', 'agents provocateurs' and all the rest of it. This is simply stupid abuse …
> People do vary in intellectual status. Why deny this in favour of the undifferentiated mass, or accede to the demand of the latter that superior brains should acquiesce in the delimitation of their political and other objectives to conciliate the mass who can see no further than their noses?[111]

In his reply Henderson raised the issue of MacDiarmid's "fascist" articles of 1923. As we have seen, this simply muddied the waters. They then got bogged down in a tussle about Henderson's translation of Gramsci, in which MacDiarmid showed that he had a good grasp of the ideas of the Italian Marxist.[112] But the "flyting" failed to clarify the argument between the two men about elitism.

The Most Mediocre Thing

MacDiarmid explained his position more fully in *A Political Speech,* an address he gave to the 1320 Club in April 1968, and also in book reviews in *Catalyst* of H.J. Paton's *The Claim of Scotland* and H.J. Hanham's *Scottish Nationalism.* He considered that the best thing about the SNP was the many young people in its ranks, but they had never been, "put in possession of their national heritage" because of an English dominated educational system.

> It is because too many people in the National Party have no concern with the things of fundamental importance, with the great spiritual issues underlying the mere statistics of trade and industry, with the ends to which all other things should be means, that I don't feel the destiny of Scotland lies with it. At present they are anxious above all not to go too far, they deprecate Anglophobia, many do not envisage armed action. Well no one in his senses wants warfare, but if we are determined to be absolutely independent, it may be and almost certainly will be forced upon us.[113]

In his review of Paton he expanded on his concept of democracy,

> Plebiscitary "democracy" can never determine what Scotland "really wants" – or rather needs, a very different matter – and the S.N.P. 's 100,000 membership, consisting largely of Poujadists, philistines and mean spirited careerists, is obviously no court of appeal to which the matter can be reasonably referred…. The fact is that thanks to the virtual monopoly given in Scottish schools and universities over the past two and a half centuries, almost the whole of our population has been deracinated and has no knowledge at all of Scottish literature, history or our native languages.[114]

He repeated this criticism of the SNP in his review of Hanham's book, its members were "English educated" and their "political, economic and other ideas move within the framework of English party politics." The problem for Scotland was mediocrity, and this stemmed from the Act of Union, which was "the most mediocre thing the rulers of Scotland ever did."[115]

What he meant by an "elite" was not, as Hamish Henderson had charged, an exclusive group based on secrecy and privilege. It was a Platonic cadre of philosopher rulers who understood the principles that lie behind the superficial appearances, with which most minds are satisfied. He did not believe that Scotland could be freed, in any meaningful sense, unless it recaptured the culture and history that had been buried under the Union. Only those who had thoroughly absorbed and understood this culture could lead the nation to freedom.

The Great Spiritual Issues

One of the clichés about MacDiarmid is that he was contradictory. But *A Political Speech* showed how little his political thinking had changed during more than four decades. He was, as he had always been, a utopian. He still believed that only a Platonic elite could revive Scottish culture. And he denounced,

> ... those Anglo-Scots intellectuals who bleat of a false antithesis, internationalism not nationalism, as if it were possible to have one without the other. They sin against the universal law of life which invests life in individuals not conglomerations.[116]

A nationalist party based on popular support, with little interest in sophisticated ideas or culture, had occupied the space he had reserved, in his own mind, for a national movement that could turn Scotland into the nation of his imagination. But he did not conclude that he had been wrong, he believed that it was Scotland's intellectual and political leaders, and its national movement, that had failed.

This was his last important political battle, the 1320 Club disintegrated, *Catalyst* and *Sgian Dubh* ceased publication, the splinter groups faded away and the SNP was left in undisputed leadership of the nationalist movement. MacDiarmid died in 1978 and he did not witness the humiliating result of the 1979 devolution referendum, to which he would have responded, "I told you so." But if the nation had achieved independence from Westminster rule during his lifetime, he would still have regarded that as a wretched compromise.

MacDiarmid's revolt was in the name of a future Scotland which could only be grasped partially and intuitively, which is why his political thinking was fundamentally utopian. He looked for the essence of Scotland in its European (particularly its French) links, which had been broken by the Union. He sought it in the country's Catholic past, in the fragments of its Lowland language, in its Gaelic heritage, in the influx of Celtic Irish, in its social radicalism, and in its literary renaissance. He strove to unite them in a revolutionary new synthesis but, in the end, his extremes never did meet.

Notes

1. *Complete Poems,* Vol. I, pp. 603–4.
2. See Susan R. Wilson (ed.), *The Correspondence Between Hugh MacDiarmid and Sorley MacLean: An Annotated Edition*, Edinburgh University Press, 2010, p. 186.
3. *Ibid.*, p. 188.
4. *Letters,* p. 195.
5. *Ibid.*, p. 184.
6. Oliver Brown "The Scottish Socialist Party", *Catalyst* Spring 1949.
7. *Scots Socialist* June 1942.
8. Stephen Howe *Anti-Colonialism in British Politics. The Left and the End of Empire 1918–64,* Oxford, Clarendon Press, 1993, p. 115.
9. For accounts of the SNP during these years see Brand (1978) pp. 237–42, Finlay (1994) pp. 206–43 & McCormick (19555) pp. 96–113.
10. For a discussion of Scottish and Welsh alienation during the war, over conscription and English cultural insensitivity, see Sonya O. Rose, *Which People's War, National Identity and Citizenship in Britain 1939–45, Oxford University Press,* 2003, pp. 218–38.
11. *Scottish News and Comment* No. 8, July 1939.
12. NLS Acc. 3721/2/30.
13. Arthur Donaldson, *Scotland's Tomorrow. Our Fight to Live,* Glasgow, Scottish Secretariat, 1946, p. 20.
14. *New Selected Letters*, p. 192.
15. See his criticisms of socialism in *Scottish News and Comment* No. 14, January 1940 & *Scotland's Tomorrow* p. 12.
16. Scots Independent September 1939.
17. See for example *Scottish News and Comment* No. 8. July 1939 and the *Scots Socialist* January-February 1942.
18. *New Selected Letters* pp. 200–6.
19. See the histories of Scottish Nationalism, cited above.
20. *The National Movement in Scotland,* p. 278.
21. *Ibid.,* p. 278.
22. *Ibid.,* p. 250.
23. *Ibid.,* p. 67.
24. NLS Ms. 27203.
25. *Ibid.*

26. NLS Ms. 10090/6.

27. *Raucle Tongue, The III*, p. 113.

28. *National Weekly* 4th. February 1950.

29. For discussions of the Covenant movement see the histories of Scottish nationalism cited above, and James Mitchell, *Strategies For Self-Government: The Campaigns For a Scottish Parliament*. Edinburgh Polygon, 1996, pp 144–8.

30. See reproduction in Gordon Wright, *Hugh MacDiarmid an Illustrated Biography,* Gordon Wright Publishing, Edinburgh, 1977, pp. 86–7.

31. *Raucle Tongue, The III*, p. 214.

32. *Raucle Tongue, The III*, p. 216.

33. *National Weekly* 4th March 1950.

34. NLS Ms. 27203.

35. *National Weekly* Election Supplement, Kelvingrove Edition, n.d. in NLS Ms. 27208.

36. Neal Wood, *Communism and British Intellectuals*, London, Gollancz, 1959, p. 160.

37. *Scots Independent* August 1945.

38. *Scots Independent* May 1946.

39. See, *Convention of Delegates of the Resistance Movements of the Anti-Bolshevik Nations of Europe and Asia. Held in Edinburgh on 12th, 13th, and 14th June 1950.* Edinburgh, Scottish League for European Freedom, 1950.

40. See Douglas Macleod, *Morningside Mata Haris, How MI6 deceived Scotland's Great and Good,* Edinburgh, Birlinn, 2005, p. 85 *passim.*

41. *Scottish Journal* No.5, January 1953.

42. *Scots Independent* September 1950.

43. *Scots Independent* November 1950.

44. *New Selected Letters* p. 258.

45. *Letters* p. 269.

46. *New Selected Letters* p. 289.

47. *Communism and British Intellectuals*, London, Gollancz, 1959, p. 158.

48. See, for example, John Gollan, *Scottish Prospect*, Glasgow, 1948, pp. 210–28.

49. Scottish Congress for Friendship and Co-operation with the U.S.S.R., *Scotland the USSR and the Future, Official Report of the Scottish Congress for Friendship and Co-operation with the U.S.S.R.*, Glasgow, June 16–17th 1945, p. 14.

50. *Scotland-USSR Society 1945–1985: 40 years working for friendship : a brief account. Glasgow,* Scotland-USSR Society, 1985.

51. Stanley Roger Green, *A Clanjamfray of Poets a tale of Literary Edinburgh,* Edinburgh, The Saltire Society, 2007, p. 10.

52. Minutes of the Executive Committee of the Scotland-USSR Society, 27/12/47, TD1125/1/1, Glasgow City Archives, Mitchell Library, Glasgow.

53. *Raucle Tongue, The III*, pp. 363–4.

54. *Raucle Tongue, The III*, p. 362.

55. *MacDiarmid,* p. 410.

56. John Saville *The Socialist Register 1976*, pp. 1–23 http://www.marxists.org/archive/saville/1976/xx/20-cpgb.htm.

57. NLS Ms. 27158, he meant, of course, "intra-party" and not "inter-party".

58. *Raucle Tongue, The III*, p. 362.

59. Hamish Henderson, *The Armstrong Nose Selected Letters of Hamish Henderson*, Edited by Alec Finlay, Edinburgh, Polygon, 1996, p. 95.

60. NLS Ms. 27435/170 f.44. I am grateful to John Manson for providing me with a copy of this document.

61. *Raucle Tongue, The III*, p. 259.

62. *Ibid.*
63. *New Selected Letters* p. 273.
64. Georg von Rauch,, *A History of Soviet Russia,* Translated by Peter & Annette Jacobson, New York, Washington & London, Praeger, Sixth Edition, 1972 p. 388.
65. *The Soviet Economy Since Stalin* 1965, p. 17.
66. *The Soviet Experiment*, p. 367.
67. "Georgians" in *The Nationalities Question in the Soviet Union*, p.185.
68. David Caute, *The Dancer Defects. The Struggle for Cultural Supremacy during the Cold War,* Oxford University Press, 2003, p. 1.
69. *New Selected Letters, p. 278.*
70. *Raucle Tongue, The III*, pp.395–6. Of course, Calder was mistaken about Pasternak, who was not executed, nor even arrested. But it was touch and go. Stalin is reputed to have spared him with the words, "leave that cloud dweller in peace". See Vitaly Shentalinsky *The KGB's Literary Archive,* London, Harvill Press, 1995, p.149.
71. *New Selected Letters* pp. 494–6.
72. *Raucle Tongue, The III*, pp. 142–5.
73. William D. Stansfield, Biological Sciences Department, California Polytechnic State University, "Luther Burbank: Honorary Member of the American Breeders' Association", http://jhered.oxfordjournals.org/cgi/content/full/97/2/95, 11/08/08
74. For details of Mirsky's life and his relationship with MacDiarmid see, G. S. Smith, *D. S. Mirsky, a Russian Life,* Oxford University Press, 2000 & G. S. Smith, "D. S. Mirskii and Hugh MacDiarmid: A Relationship and an Exchange of Letters," *Slavonica,* Vol. 3, No. 2, 1996/7, pp. 49–60.
75. *Scots Independent* July 1945, (italics in original).
76. *Letters* p. 622.
77. *Ibid.*
78. *Letters* pp. 619–20.
79. *Letters* p. 619.
80. *New Selected Letters* pp. 275–6.
81. Alan Bold (ed.) *The Thistle Rises. An Anthology of Poetry and Prose, by Hugh MacDiarmid*, London, Hamish Hamilton, 1984, p. 227.
82. *Raucle Tongue, The II*, p. 470.
83. *Raucle Tongue, The III*, p. 442.
84. *Ibid.*, p. 443.
85. *New Selected Letters* p. 491.
86. *Ibid., p. 523.*
87. Christopher Harvie, *Scotland and Nationalism,* London and New York Routledge, Second Edition, 1994, p. 173.
88. *Selected Essays* pp. 230–1.
89. John Herdman has given a vivid description of the movement in these years in his *Poets, Pubs and Pillar Boxes. Memoirs of an era in Scottish Politics and Letters,* Kirkcaldy, Akros Publications, 1999.
90. *Letters* p. 874, "1320" commemorated the date of the *Declaration of Arbroath*, the Scottish appeal to the Pope against the English Crown's attempts to annex their country.
91. Leaflet published by the 1320 Club advertising the event, copy in the writer's possession.
92. *'In Defens' A Pilot Outline of Scotland's Defence Requirements issued by the 1320 Club.* Currie, Midlothian, The 1320 Club, n.d. (1968), p. 12.
93. See Andrew Murray Scott and Iain Macleay, *Britain's Secret War. tartan Terrorism and the Anglo-American State,* Edinburgh, Mainstream, 1990, pp. 194–5. Derek Boothby was a cousin of the Conservative politician Robert Boothby.

94. Interview with Randall Foggie, Kirkcaldy, 26th August 2011. "EIIR referred to the title "Elizabeth the Second" which the new Queen had adopted, to the distress of many Scots who regarded it as a claim that Scotland had been part of England at the time of the first Elizabeth.

95. *Poets, Pubs and Pillar Boxes,* p. 24.

96. The first issues were misspelt "Skian Dubh".

97. *Scots Independent* 2 March, 1968.

98. Gordon Wilson, *SNP: The Turbulent Years 1960–90,* Stirling, Scots Independent, 2009, p. 42.

99. James Halliday, *Yours for Scotland. A Memoir,* Scots Independent, 2011, p. 81.

100. *Letters* p. 874.

101. NLS Ms. 27035, *Red Scotland ms.* The author first read this passage in July 1999, on the afternoon of the day he heard Donald Dewar respond to First Minister's Questions for the first time in the Scottish Parliament, which had been opened a few days earlier.

102. *A Bill for the Government of Scotland,* Currie, Midlothian, 1320 Club, 1974.

103. *New Selected Letters,* p. 483.

104. Interview 26th August 2011.

105. *New Selected Letters* pp. 482–4.

106. See "On *Sgian Dubh's* Fifth Birthday", *Raucle Tongue, The III,* pp. 468–71. "A Message from Hugh MacDiarmid, *Sgian Dubh, September 1973.*

107. *Letters* p. 732.

108. James Porter & Herschel Gower, *Jeannie Robertson. Emergent Singer Tranformative Voice,* East Linton, Tuckwell Press, 1995, p. 58.

109. Hamish Henderson, *The Armstrong Nose Selected Letters of Hamish Henderson,* Edited by Alec Finlay, Edinburgh, Polygon, 1996, p. 119.

110. *The Armstrong Nose* p. 164.

111. *Ibid.,* p. 165.

112. *Ibid.,* pp. 167–8.

113. *Ibid.,* p. 343.

114. *Raucle Tongue, The III,* p. 467.

115. *Catalyst* Autumn 1969.

116. *Albyn* p. 341.

Appendix

T.S.E.'S REVIEW OF ODON POR'S *FASCISM*

"The Fascist Idea." *Fascism* by Odon Por (the Labour Publishing Co. 7/6 net)

This admirably translated volume is by a long way the most systematic and satisfying exposition of Fascism which has yet appeared in English. Indeed it is likely to rank for some time as the most authoritative study of a complex subject available. The enterprise of the Labour Publishing Company in issuing it is to be highly commended.... The book shows no signs of haste, and no-one could detect untold the fact that this is a translation at all. Nor is it loosely constructed, with those tendencies to incohesion and repetition one would expect in a book written under such conditions. On the contrary is a clean-cut compact piece of work, bodying forth the whole mass of Fascist theory, achievement and tendency in a masterly and definitive fashion.

It is impossible in the space available here to adequately discuss the author's conclusions. The book is indispensable to all who are interested in international politics, the evolution of civilisation, or, more narrowly, the future of labour movements in European countries. Of particular interest to readers of "The Scottish Nation," in view of articles on Fascism and Scottish Home Rule that have appeared in these columns - and the increasing realisation that not only does the Home Rule Question depend mainly upon the Labour Movement, but the Labour Movement itself in Scotland may be consummated or retarded precisely in proportion as its leaders recognise or fail to recognise the tactical necessity (to put it no higher) at the present juncture of making political disjunction from England their first great objective instead of their incidental aim - is the convincing fashion in which the author corroborates Mr. Grieve's and Mr. Clark's contentions as to the inherent "leftism" of the Fascist movement. The Scottish M.P. s who spoke at the Scotland's Day demonstration the other week would be well advised to make a careful investigation by aid of this book of the possibilities of a Scottish Fascism.

"The origin of Fascism" says Odon Por, "and its present orientation indicate that it has no desire to oppose Labour, but aims first at reconciling Labour with the nation, and secondly, at creating a national spirit of citizenship, with Labour for its basis. Later he says, elaborating his most suggestive parallel between Russian Bolshevism and Italian Fascism, "just as orthodox revolutionaries are in Italian Fascism a purely conservative force, so do plutocrats see in Bolshevism one that is purely destructive. But the processes of history do not develop according to theoretical formulae, nor lend themselves to be neatly catalogued under a single heading; the proceed along the track that is laid out for them by economic factors. They may leave the line owing to some impediment; but if they are to advance they must inevitably return to it. The march of history in our day is along a track characterised by a combination of various methods of economic activity; its destination is that state of things in which the various economic agents will act together in unison for the public benefit. The most varied types of property and of productive organisation must be recognised, but they must be framed And incorporated in a State, functioning effectively in the collective interest, and they must be required to work together harmoniously. The precise form of this state, when it does become established, will be fixed, no doubt, by tradition in the sense that it will reflect the tendencies, institutional, mental, and temperamental of the respective countries.

The Scottish Nation
4 September, 1923

Bibliography

All the knowledge is woven in neatly
So that the plaited ends come to the hand.
Pull any of the tabs, and a sequence
Of practical information is drawn.

(From *Plaited Like the Generations of Men*)[1]

Documentary Sources

British Library of Political Science

Youth Movement Archive, KK/90.

National Library of Scotland

Acc. 3721
Acc. 5927
Acc. 6058
Dep. 209
Ms. 10090
Ms. 26035
Ms. 27203
Ms. 27158
Ms. 27035
Ms. 27435

Mitchell Library, Glasgow

Glasgow City Archives, TD1125.

University of Delaware

Ms. 225

Newspapers and Periodicals

Abundance
Attack
Daily Record
Edinburgh Evening News
Evening Times (Glasgow)
Forward
Free Man, The
Guth na Bliadhna
Left Review
Liberty
Modern Scot, The
National Weekly, The
New Scotland
Pictish Review, The
Scots Independent
Scottish Journal
Standard, The
Vanguard, The

Works of Reference

Edwards, Paul (Editor in Chief), *The Encyclopaedia of Philosophy*, 8 Vols., New York & London, Macmillan & Collier Macmillan."

Knox, William (ed.), *Scottish labour Leaders 1918–39, A Biographical Dictionary,* Edinburgh, Mainstream, 1984.

Scottish Biographies 1938, pub. by E. J. Thurston, London, Jackson, Son & Co., Ltd., Glasgow.

Published collections and editions of MacDiarmid's writings

The Correspondence Between Hugh MacDiarmid and Sorley MacLean: An Annotated Edition, Edinburgh University Press, 2010, edited by Susan R. Wilson.

The Letters of Hugh MacDiarmid, University of Georgia Press, 1984 edited by Alan Bold.

Hugh MacDiarmid, *The Thistle Rises. An Anthology of Poetry and Prose, by Hugh MacDiarmid*, London, Hamish Hamilton, 1984 edited by Alan Bold.

Hugh MacDiarmid, the Raucle Tongue. Hitherto Uncollected Prose, Vol. I, Manchester, Carcarnet, 1996; Vol. II, 1997; Vol. III, 1998 edited by Angus Calder, Glen Murray and Alan Riach.

MacDiarmid, Hugh, *Aesthetics in Scotland,* edited & Introduced by Alan Bold, Edinburgh, Mainstream, 1984.

MacDiarmid, Hugh (ed.), *The Golden Treasury of Scottish Poetry,* London, Macmillan, 1948.

MacDiarmid, Hugh, *First Hymn to Lenin and Other Poems,* London, The Unicorn Press, 1931.

MacDiarmid, Hugh, *Hugh MacDiarmid. The Revolutionary Art of the Future. Rediscovered Poems.* Manchester, Carcanet, 2003 edited by John Manson, Dorian Grieve and Alan Riach.

MacDiarmid, Hugh, *Hugh MacDiarmid, Albyn Shorter Books and Monographs,* Manchester, Carcanet, 1996, edited by Alan Riach.

MacDiarmid, Hugh, *Hugh MacDiarmid. Contemporary Scottish Studies,* Manchester 1995.

Hugh MacDiarmid Complete Poems, Vol. I, Manchester, Carcanet, 1993; Vol. II, 1994 edited by Michael Grieve and W. R. Aitken.

MacDiarmid, Hugh, *The Company I've Kept;* London, Hutchinson, 1966.

Hugh MacDiarmid's Epic Poetry, Edinburgh University Press, 1991 edited by Alan Riach.

MacDiarmid, Hugh, *Selected Essays of Hugh MacDiarmid,* Jonathan Cape, London, 1969, edited by Duncan Glen.

MacDiarmid, Hugh, *Hugh MacDiarmid. Selected Prose,* Carcanet, Manchester 1992 edited by Alan Riach.

MacDiarmid, Hugh, *Hugh MacDiarmid Lucky Poet,* Manchester, Carcanet, 1994 edited by Alan Riach.

MacDiarmid, Hugh, *Hugh MacDiarmid New Selected Letters,* Manchester, Carcanet, 2001, edited by Dorian Grieve, Owen Dudley Edwards & Alan Riach.

Interview

Randall Foggie, Kirkcaldy, 26th August 2011.

Books, Pamphlets & Articles

Angell, Sir, Norman *et al. Eleventh Hour Questions,* Edinburgh & London, The Moray Press, 1937.

Avineri, Shlomo, *The Social and Political Thought of Karl Marx,* Cambridge University Press, 1971.

Bedford, the Duke of, *The Financiers Little Game, or The Shape of Things to Come,* Glasgow, The Strickland Press, 1945.

Benson, G. R. (ed.), Richard Lewis Nettleship *Lectures on the Republic of Plato,* London, MacMillan, 1910.

Blythe, Ernest, *The State and the Language, An English version of the Presidential address of Ernest Blythe to Comhdháil Náisiúnta na Gaeilge, 3 December, 1949,* 2nd ed., Dublin, Comhdháil Náisiúnta, 1951.

Bold, Alan, *MacDiarmid. Christopher Murray Grieve. A Critical Biography,* London, John Murray, 1988.

Boutelle, Ann Edwards. *Thistle and Rose. A Study of MacDiarmid's Poetry,* MacDonald, Loanhead, 1980.

Bold, Alan, *MacDiarmid The Terrible Crystal,* London, Routledge & Kegan Paul, 1983.

Brand, Jack *The National Movement in Scotland,* Routledge & Kegan Paul London, Henley & Boston 1978.

Branson, Noreen, *History of the Communist Party of Great Britain, 1927–41,* London, Lawrence & Wishart, 1985.

Bringmann, Rudolf, *Geschichte Irlands; ein Kampf um die völkische Freiheit,* Berlin, Junker und Dünnhaupt, 1939.

Briffault, Robert, *Breakdown. The Collapse of Traditional Civilisation,* New York, Brentano, 1932, & London, Gollancz, 1935.

Brown, Terence, *Ireland a Social and Cultural History,* London, Fontana, 1981.

Buhle, Paul, *Marxism in the United States: Remapping the History of the American Left,* London, Verso, 1987.

Cahm, Eric, "Revolt, Conservatism and Reaction in Paris 1905–25," in Malcolm Bradbury & James McFarlane (eds.), *Modernism 1890–1930,* Penguin, Harmondsworth, 1991, pp. 162–71.

Caute, David, *The Dancer Defects. The Struggle for Cultural Supremacy during the Cold War,* Oxford University Press, 2003.

Cole, GDH, *Guild Socialism,* London, The Fabian Society, 1920.

Cole, GDH, *Money its Present and Future,* 3rd. edn., London, Toronto, Melbourne & Sydney, Cassell, 1947.

Craik, William W., *The Central Labour College, 109–29. A Chapter in the History of Working-class Education, London, Lawrence & Wishart, 1964.*

Craigie, W. A., John Buchan, Peter Giles & J. M. Bulloch, *The Scottish Tongue,* London, Toronto & Melbourne, Cassell & Co., 1924.

Croft, Andy (ed) *A Weapon in the Struggle. The Cultural History of the Communist Party in Britain.* London & Sterling Virginia, Pluto Press, 1998.

Davis, Alex & Lee M. Jenkins, *Locations of Literary Modernism, Region and Nation in British and American Modernist Poetry,* Cambridge University Press, 2000.

Degras, Jane, (ed.) *The Communist International 1919–43, Documents,* Vol. I, New Impression, London, Frank Cass, 1971. Vol. III, Oxford University Press, 1965.

Delzell, Charles F. (ed.), *Mediterranean Fascism 1919–1945,* London, The Macmillan Press, 1971.

Dobb, Maurice, *Social Credit Discredited,* London, Martin Lawrence, 1936.

Donaldson, Arthur, *Scotland's Tomorrow. Our Fight to Live,* Glasgow, Scottish Secretariat, 1946.

Douglas, C. H., *The Alberta Experiment,* Eyre & Spottiswood, London, 1937.

Douglas, C. H., *Economic Democracy,* London, Cecil Palmer, Third Edition, 1928.

Douglas, C. H., *The Nature of Democracy*, London, Stanley Nott, 1934.

Douglas, C. H. *Social Credit*, London, C. Palmer, 1924.

Douglas, C. H., *Warning Democracy,* London, C. M. Grieve, 1931.

Douglas, C. H. & A. R. Orage, *Credit Power and Democracy*, London, Cecil Palmer, 1920.

Drakeford, Mark, *Social Movements and their Supporters. The Green Shirts in England*, Basingstoke & New York, MacMillan, 1997.

Durbin, Elizabeth, *New Jerusalems. The Labour Party and the Economics of Democratic Socialism*, Routledge & Kegan Paul, London, Boston, Melbourne & Henley, 1985.

Durbin, Evan, *Socialism and "Social Credit"*, London, The Labour Party, 1935.

Durbin, Evan*, The Politics of Democratic Socialism*, London, George Routledge & Sons, 1940.

Duval K. D., & Sydney Goodsir Smith (eds.), *Hugh MacDiarmid a Festschrift,* Edinburgh, K. D. Duval, 1962.

Erskine, Ruairidh of Mar, *Changing Scotland* , Montrose, The Review Press, 1931.

Evans, Gwynfor, *For the Sake of Wales the Memoirs of Gwynfor Evans*, translated from the Welsh by Meic Stephens, Cardiff, Welsh Academic Press, 1996.

Ferguson, Aitken, *Scotland,* Glasgow, the Communist Party of Great Britain (Scottish District Committee), 1938.

Ferris William, *The Gaelic Commonwealth: Being the Political and Economic Programme for the Irish Progressive Party.* Dublin: Talbot Press, 1923.

Figgis, Darrell, *The Gaelic State in the Past and the Future, or "The Crown of a Nation",* Dublin, Maunsel & Co, 1917.

Finlay, John L., *Social Credit the English Origins*, London & Montreal, McGill - Queen's University Press, 1972.

Finlay, Richard J., *Independent and Free: Scottish Politics and the Origins of the Scottish National Party 1918–1945*, Edinburgh, John Donald, c1994.

Finlay, Richard, *Modern Scotland, 1914–2000,* London, Profile Books, 2004.

Fishman, Nina, *The British Communist Party and the Trade Unions 1933–45,* Aldershot, Scoular Press, 1995.

Foote, Geoffrey, *The Labour Party's Political Thought A History,* Basingstoke & London, Macmillan, 3rd edition, 1997.

Fyrth, Jim, (ed.), *Britain, Fascism and the Popular Front* London, Lawrence & Wishart, 1985.

Gaitskell, Hugh, "Four Monetary Heretics" in G. D. H. Cole (ed.) *What Everybody Wants to Know About Money*, London, Gollancz, 1933.

Gaitskell, Hugh, *Money and Everyday Life,* London, Labour Book Service, *n.d.* [*circa 1939*].

Gaitskell, Hugh, Evan Durbin and W. R. Hiskett *Socialist Credit Policy*, London, New Fabian Research Bureau & Victor Gollancz, 2nd ed., 1936.

Gallagher, Tom, *Glasgow the Uneasy Peace. Religious Tension in Modern Scotland, 1818–1914,* Manchester University Press, 1987.

Gibbon, Lewis Grassic & Hugh MacDiarmid (eds.) *Scottish Scene*, London, Hutchinson & Co., 1934.

Gish, Nancy K. (ed.), *Hugh MacDiarmid Man and Poet,* Maine, National Poetry Foundation & Edinburgh University Press, 1992.

Gollan, John, *Scottish Prospect*, Glasgow, 1948.

Gorgolini, Pietro, *The Fascist Movement in Italian Life*, Edited with Introduction by M. D. Petre, London, T. Fisher Unwin Ltd., 1923.

Graham, Laurence & Brian Smith (eds.), *MacDiarmid in Shetland*, Lerwick, Shetland Library, 1992.

Green, Stanley Roger, *A Clanjamfray of Poets a tale of Literary Edinburgh*, Edinburgh, The Saltire Society, 2007.

Griffin, Roger, *The Nature of Fascism*, Routledge. London & New York, 1994,

Halliday, James, *Yours for Scotland. A Memoir*, Scots Independent, 2011.

Hanham, H. J., *Scottish Nationalism*, London, Faber and Faber, 1969.

Harvie, Christopher, *Scotland and Nationalism*, London and New York, Routledge, Second Edition, 1994.

Henderson, Hamish, *The Armstrong Nose Selected Letters of Hamish Henderson*, Edited by Alec Finlay, Edinburgh, Polygon, 1996.

Herbert, W. N., *To Circumjack MacDiarmid. The Poetry and Prose of Hugh MacDiarmid*, Oxford, Clarendon Press, 1992.

Herdman, John, *Poets, Pubs and Pillar Boxes. Memoirs of an era in Scottish Politics and Letters*, Kirkcaldy, Akros Publications, 1999.

Holton, Bob, *British Syndicalism 1900–1914. Myths and Realities*, London, Pluto, 1976.

Hook, Sidney, *From Hegel to Marx; Studies in the Intellectual Development of Karl Marx*, New York, Reynal & Hitchcock 1936.

Howe, Stephen, *Anti-Colonialism in British Politics. The Left and the End of Empire 1918–64*, Oxford, Clarendon Press, 1993.

Howe, Stephen, *Ireland and Empire. Colonial Legacies in Irish History and Culture*, Oxford University Press, 2000.

Howell, David, *British Workers and the Independent Labour Party*, Manchester University Press, 1983.

Keating, Michael and David Bleiman, *Labour and Scottish Nationalism*, London & Basingstoke, MacMillan, 1979.

Kendall, Walter, *The Revolutionary Movement in Britain 1900–21. The Origins of British Communism*, London, Weidenfield & Nicholson, 1969, reprinted 1971.

Keynes, John Maynard, *General Theory of Employment Interest and Money*, Macmillan, London, 1936.

Kenny, Michael, *The First New Left. British Intellectuals After Stalin*, London, Lawrence & Wishart, 1995.

Kristjánsdóttir, Ragenheiður, "Communists and the National Question in Scotland and Iceland", c. 1930 to c. 1940", *The Historical Journal*, Vol. 45, No. 3, 2002, pp. 601–18.

International Centre for Fascist Studies, *A Survey of Fascism the Year Book of the International Centre for Fascist Studies*, Vol. 1, London, Ernest Benn, 1928.

Kołakowski, Leszek, *Main Currents of Marxism*, (One volume edition), Book One *The Founders*, Book Two *The Golden Age*, Book Three *The Breakdown*, New York & London, W.W. Norton & Co., c2005.

Laybourn, Keith & Dylan Murphy *Under the Red Flag, A History of Communism in Britain c.1848–1991*, Stroud, Sutton Publishing, 1999.

Leneman, Leah, *Land Fit for Heroes? Land Settlement in Scotland After World War I,* Aberdeen University Press, 1989.

Lynch, David, *Radical Politics in Modern Ireland. The Irish Socialist Republican Party 1896–1904,* Dublin & Portland Oregon, Irish Academic Press, 2005.

Lynch, Peter, *SNP, The History of the Scottish National Party*, Cardiff, Welsh Academic Press, 2002.

Linklater, Andro, *Compton Mackenzie a Life*, London, Hogarth Press, 1992.

Lyall, Scott & Margery Palmer McCulloch, (eds.), The Edinburgh Companion to Hugh MacDiarmid, Edinburgh University Press, 2011.

Lyttleton, Adrian (ed.) *Italian Fascisms from Pareto to Gentile*, London, Cape, 1973.

Manson, John, "The Poet and the Party" *Cencrastus no. 65,* n.d.

Margolies, David (ed.) *Writing the Revolution, Cultural Criticism from Left Review,* London, Chicago & Illinois, Pluto, 1998.

Marr, Andrew, *The Making of Modern Britain,* London, Macmillan, 2009.

Martin, Wallace, *The New Age Under Orage*, Manchester University Press & New York, Barnes & Noble, 1967.

Maume, Patrick, *The Long Gestation: Irish Nationalist Life, 1891–1918*, Dublin, Gill & Macmillan, 1999.

Miller, Karl (ed.), *Memoirs of a Modern Scotland,* London, Faber & Faber, 1970.

Milton, Nan (ed.), *John MacLean, In the Rapids of Revolution*, London, Alison & Busby, 1978.

Mitchell, James, *Strategies For Self-Government: The Campaigns For a Scottish Parliament*, Edinburgh, Polygon, 1996.

Morgan, Kevin, *Against Fascism and War. Ruptures and Continuities in British Communist Politics 1935–41,* Manchester University Press, 1987.

Murray, H. M. (H. M. M.) *An Outline of Social Credit*, London, New Age Press, 1929. London, C. M. Grieve, 1931.

Muir, Willa, *Belonging a Memoir,* London, The Hogarth Press, 1968.

McCarey, Peter, *Hugh MacDiarmid and the Russians,* Scottish Academic Press, Edinburgh, 1987.

Mac Colla, Fionn, (T. J. Douglas MacDonald), *Too long in this condition. Ro fhada mar so a tha mi,* Thurso, J. Humphries, 1975.

MacCormick, John, *The Flag in the Wind, The Story of the National Movement in Scotland,* London, Victor Gollancz, 1955.

McCulloch, Margery Palmer, (ed.) *Modernism and Nationalism: Literature and Society in Scotland 1918–1939, Source Documents for the Scottish Renaissance,* Glasgow, The Association for Scottish Literary Studies, 2004.

Macintyre, Stuart, *Little Moscows, Communism and Working-class Militancy in Inter-war Britain,* London, Croom Helm, 1980.

Mackenzie, Compton, *My Life and Times, Octave Six, 1923–1930,* London, Chatto & Windus, 1967.

McLean, Iain, *The Legend of Red Clydeside,* Edinburgh, John Donald, 1983.

McLelland, J. S., (ed.), *The French Right From De Maistre to Maurras*, London, Cape, 1970.

Macleod, Douglas, *Morningside Mata Haris, How MI6 deceived Scotland's Great and Good,* Edinburgh, Birlinn, 2005.

McMillan, James F, *Twentieth Century France. Politics and Society 1898– 1991.* London, New York, Melbourne, Auckland, Edward Arnold, 1992.

MacPherson, C. B., *Democracy in Alberta,* University of Toronto Press, 1953.

McShane, Harry & Joan Smith, *Harry McShane. No Mean Fighter,* London, Pluto, 1978.

Nairn, Tom, *The Break-Up of Britain, Crisis and Neo-Nationalism,* London, NLB, 1977.

Nolte, Ernst, *Three Faces of Fascism; Action Francais Italian Fascism, National Socialism.,* Holt, Rinehart and Winston, New York 1966.

Normand, Tom, *The Modern Scot. Modernism and Nationalism in Scottish Art 1928–1955,* Aldershot, Ashgate Publishing Ltd., 2000.

O'Duffy, Eimar, "The Leisure State" in *The Modern Scot,* August 1932, pp. 155 – 62.

Orage, A. R. (ed.), *National Guilds, an Enquiry into the Wage System and a Way Out,* London, G. Bell & Sons.

Orwell, George, *Inside the Whale and Other Essays*, Penguin, Harmondsworth, 1957.

Paton, H. J., *The Claim of Scotland* , Aberdeen University Press, 1968.

Phelps, Christopher, *Young Sidney Hook, Marxist and Pragmatist,* Ithaca & London, Cornell University Press, 1997.

Plato, *The Republic,* Translated by AD Lindsay, London, Everyman's Library, New Edition 1976.

Por, Odon, *Fascism,* Translated by Emily Townshend, [American edition], New York, A. Knopf, 1923.

Porter, James & Herschel Gower, *Jeannie Robertson. Emergent Singer Tranformative Voice,* East Linton, Tuckwell Press, 1995.

Powell, Lieut. Col. Arthur E., *The Deadlock of Finance,* London, Cecil Palmer, 2nd. ed. 1931.

Rauch, Georg von, *A History of Soviet Russia,* Translated by Peter & Annette Jacobson, New York, Washington & London, Praeger, Sixth Edition, 1972.

Redman, Tim, *Ezra Pound and Italian Fascism*, Cambridge University Press, 1991.

Redman, Tim, "Por, Odon," in Tryphonopoulos and Adams (eds.), *The Ezra Pound Encyclopedia*, Westport Connecticut & London, Greenwood Press, 2005.

Rée, Jonathan, *Proletarian Philosophers. Problems in Socialist Culture in Britain, 1900–1940,* Oxford, Clarendon, 1984.

Robin, Martin, *Shades of Right, Nativist and Fascist Politics in Canada 1920– 1940*, University of Toronto Press, 1992.

Rossi, A., *A Communist Party in Action. An Account of the Organization and Operations in France,* tr. by Wilmoore Kendall, New Haven, Yale University Press, 1949.

Salamone, William (ed.) *Italy From the Risorgimento to Fascism*, Newton Abbot, David & Charles, 1971.

Schwarz, Harry, *The Soviet Economy Since Stalin*, London, Gollancz, 1965.

Scotland-USSR Society, *Scotland-USSR Society 1945–1985: 40 Years Working For Friendship: a Brief Account. Glasgow*, Scotland-USSR Society, 1985.

Scott, P. H. and A. C. Davis, *The Age of MacDiarmid*, Edinburgh, Mainstream, 1980.

Scottish Congress for Friendship and Co-operation with the U.S.S.R., *Scotland the USSR and the Future*, Official Report of the Scottish Congress for Friendship and Co-operation with the U.S.S.R., Glasgow, June 16–17th 1945, p. 14.

Selver, Paul, *Orage and the New Age Circle*. George Allen and Unwin, London, 1959.

Stingel, Janine, *Social Discredit. Social Credit and the Jewish Response*, Montreal, McGill-Queen's University Press, 2000.

Smith, G. S., *D. S. Mirsky, a Russian Life*, Oxford University Press, 2000.

Smith, G. S., "D. S. Mirskii and Hugh MacDiarmid: A Relationship and an Exchange of Letters," *Slavonica*, Vol. 3, No. 2, 1996/7, pp. 49–60.

Smith, Graham (ed.) *The Nationalities Question in the Soviet Union*, London & New York, Longman, 1990.

Spence, Lewis, *Freedom for Scotland. The Case for Scottish Self-Government*, Edinburgh, The Scottish National Movement, n.d. [1927].

Spengler, Oswald, *The Decline of the West. Form and Actuality*. Authorised translation with notes by Charles Francis Atkinson, New York, Alfred A. Knopf, Vol. 1, 1927, Vol. 2, 1928.

Stalin, J. V., *Leninism*, Eden & Cedar Paul, (trans.), London, Modern Books, 2nd impression, 1932, Vol. 1.

Sunter, Ronald M., "The Rise of Scottish Nationalism in the Nineteenth Century", in *Scottish Tradition*, Canadian Association for Scottish Studies, Vol. VI, 1976, pp. 14–26.

Suny, Ronald Grigor, *The Soviet Experiment. Russia, the USSR and the Successor States*, Oxford University Press, 1998.

Thayer, George, *The British Political Fringe, a Profile*, London, Anthony Blond, 1965.

Thomas, Hugh, *The Spanish Civil War*, London, Eyre & Spottiswood, 1961, reprinted 1962.

Thompson, Willie, *The Good Old Cause, British Communism 1920–1991*, London, Pluto, 1992.

Thomson, George Malcolm, *Caledonia or the Future of the Scots*, Kegan Paul, Trench, Trübner and Co., London and New York, 1927.

Turner, Arthur, *Scottish Home Rule*, Oxford, Blackwell, 1952.

Villiers, Brougham, *England and the New Era*, London, T. Fisher Unwin, 1920.

Walker, Graham, *Intimate Strangers. Political and Cultural Interaction Between Scotland and Ulster in Modern Times*, Edinburgh, John Donald, 1995.

Wanliss, T. D., *Bars to British Unity*, Edinburgh, Scottish Home Rule Association, 1895, (Reprint).

Warrington, Marnie Hughes, *Fifty Key Thinkers on History*, London & New York, Routledge, 2000.

Weber, Eugene, *The Nationalist Revival in France, 1905–1914,* University of California Press, Berkeley & Los Angeles, 1968.

Webb Sidney and Beatrice, *Soviet Communism a New Civilisation,* Liphook, Hampshire, the authors, 1935.

Webber, G. C., *The Ideology of the British Right 1918–1939*, London & Sydney, Croom Helm, 1986.

Whyte, J. H. (ed), *Towards a New Scotland. Being a Selection from The Modern Scot,* London, Alexander Maclehose, 1935.

Wilson, Gordon, *SNP: The Turbulent Years 1960–90,* Stirling, Scots Independent, 2009.

Wintringham, T. H., "Who is for Liberty?" *Left Review*, Vol. 1, No. 2, September 1935.

Wood, Neal, *Communism and British Intellectuals*, London, Gollancz, 1959.

Wright, Gordon, *MacDiarmid an Illustrated Biography*, Edinburgh, Gordon Wright, 1977.

Young, Douglas C. C., *The Free Minded Scot. Trial of Douglas Young in the High Court Edinburgh*, Glasgow, Scottish Secretariat, n.d. [1942].

Young, James D., "Marxism and the Scottish National Question", *Journal of Contemporary History,* Vol. 18, No. 1, January 1983, pp. 141–6.

Notes

1. *Complete Poems,* Vol. II, *op. cit,* p. 872.

Index